Strategies for New Churches

HARPER'S MINISTERS PAPERBACK LIBRARY

Strategies
for New Churches

Ezra Earl Jones

Published in San Francisco by

HARPER & ROW, PUBLISHERS

New York, Hagerstown, San Francisco, London

Library of Congress Cataloging in Publication Data
Jones, Ezra Earl.
    Strategies for new churches.

    Bibliography: p. 177
    1. Church development, New. I. Title.
BV652.24.J66 1976   254   75-36731
ISBN 0-06-064184-3

84 85 86   10 9 8 7 6 5 4 3

To
Ezra, Eunice, Herbert, and Nellie Mae
and to
Drew and Camilla

Contents

Preface

A community without a church is a body without a soul, or an explorer without a compass. A church, on the other hand, cannot exist apart from a community. It is an institution created within the community to fulfill a special function. Churches are developed as communities develop.

This book is about the formation of communities and the development of Christian congregations. It deals with how communities grow, under what conditions, and how they differ. It also discusses the need for churches, why they are organized, how they vary by style of ministry and the characteristics of their members, and how they are developed. The primary focus is on how new churches may be designed appropriately for the communities they will serve.

The book is written in the belief that new church development is an urgent task today for the denominations that make up American Christianity. Regional population growth, population shifts, and the ever-changing make-up of neighborhoods and communities require new churches and redeveloped churches in those denominations that want to maintain an effective witness to Christian faith and action.

The work is divided into two parts. Part I attempts to construct a historical, theological, and sociological framework as a context in which future new churches may be developed. I propose a theological rationale for new church development and sociological principles, including a typology of churches, which are based on empirical data and contemporary theories of social organizations.

Part II deals with the process of starting new churches—the questions of what, when, where, and how. Here I discuss the step-by-step mechanics of establishing and organizing a new congregation. Chapters 5 through 12 discuss the process in sequence from the planning of a general church strategy for a metropolitan area through site selection, conducting a feasibility study, writing the mission design, securing financing for the congregation, securing the first pastor, surveying the community, gathering members, constituting the church, and construction of the first unit of a building (if one is to be built).

Sometimes existing congregations can be redeveloped as "new" congregations. Through clustering, merger, relocation, or internal transformation a new church may be established on the base of an old one. Chapter 13 explores the alternatives open to churches in decline and the conditions under which renewal can occur.

The book was written for those who are involved in or care about the development of new churches (and redevelopment of old ones that can become new): denominational executives; district, association, synod, presbytery, diocesan, and conference committees; clergy, lay leaders, and lay persons of new congregations; and all interested Christians who are concerned about the shape of the church tomorrow if we do not do a good job today in exploring new possibilities and creating churches that "fit" their communities. Some of these are people who have been critical of past new church development efforts. We agree that lessons have been learned and we do not need to repeat mistakes. Some are concerned about overemphasis on buildings. We will think about that also. Others are minorities and church people with special interest in declining churches in older neighborhoods. We hear you; the next round of new church development activity must be related to the redevelopment of existing congregations.

Christian congregations are more than social organizations. They are groups of people who share a common faith in God and are committed to his leading. This book was written in the firm belief that churches are His, that He calls them into being, and that faithful congregations are developed as loyal Christians are open to His call and guidance. The information and guidelines included here were gleaned from observing the past attempts of God's people to express their faithfulness and through prayerful reflection on the purpose of the church today and in the future. The learnings and insights are presented in the hope that all who use them will do so under the continuing correcting revelation of the Holy Spirit.

I am grateful to many people for their assistance in the preparation of this volume. My colleagues in the Church Development Task Force of the Joint Strategy and Action Committee (a coalition of the national mission agencies of mainline Protestant denominations) have given valuable advice, and many have worked with me to provide individual denominational manuals to supplement this volume and make it more useful in the churches of their respective denominations. They are James Anderson (Episcopal Church), Harold Byers (United Presbyterian Church in the U.S.A.), John DeBoer (United Church of Christ), William Hanson (American Lutheran Church), Lonnie Hass (Christian Church-Disciples of Christ), Frederick Marks (Lutheran Church in America), Clyde McCants (Associate Reformed Presbyterian Church), Glenn Orr (American Baptist Churches), Robert Rea (Presbyterian Church in the U.S.), Russell Redeker (Reformed Church in America), F. J. Redford (Southern Baptist Convention), and George Williams (United Methodist Church).

Others who read the manuscript and commented helpfully are James Davis, Ned Dewire, Jesse DeWitt, Philip Park, and Robert Wilson. The manuscript was edited by Edward Lacy and John Shopp and typed by Diona Thomas.

I am indebted to the staff and members of the new churches with whom I have worked over the past decade who have shared their experiences with me. It is their knowledge and experience that I have been privileged to share in these pages. Special thanks goes to the one who has taught me most in the field of new church development and who is now successfully involved in the development of a new congregation in Fort Myers, Florida—James R. Maxfield. I have been particularly dependent upon his experience and insights with regard to financing, gathering, and organizing new congregations. H. Paul Smith, now a local church pastor in Geneva, Nebraska, contributed many of the helpful guidelines included in chapter 12.

My always helpful and loving wife, Mary, contributed the maps and charts and much, much more. The book is dedicated to our parents who gave us a Christian heritage strengthened by their faithfulness and love, and to our children who we hope have received an equally inspired faith from us.

EZRA EARL JONES

PART I

The Framework

1: The Context of New Congregational Development Today

This book is based on four primary assumptions:

1. New churches[1] will continue to be needed as long as new communities[2] are established.

2. Protestant Christian denominations have a responsibility to assist local communities to: (a) organize new churches, including racial and ethnic congregations, (b) experiment with alternative models of congregational

---

1. The terms *church, local church,* and *congregation* are used synonymously to designate a group of people who live or participate in the same community, share similar religious beliefs, and are intentionally organized as a social institution for the purpose of pursuing the goals and participating in the rites and activities associated with their religion. The term *Church* (capitalized), except when modified by a denominational title, refers to the mystical body of persons in all ages and of all denominations who have attached the name Christian.

A "new" church is a group of people who share a common community and religious beliefs, the majority of whom have recently banded together for the first time to organize for the purpose of practicing their religion.

2. The term *community* refers to a geographical area in which people live and share some common characteristics. The area may be a comparatively small populated district possessing some quality that distinguishes it from other areas (a neighborhood), or an extensive territory such as a city, county, or metropolitan area.

style, (c) recognize human and cultural diversity in the new institutions, (d) eliminate racism, paternalism, and traditionalism, which lead to stagnation, (e) cooperate ecumenically, and (f) relate new churches to existing congregations and ministries.

3. The creation of a new church offers fresh and unique opportunities for Christians to express their faithfulness—to rethink the theology of the church and its purpose, to provide models for Christian community and service, and to reach out in evangelistic recruitment of the non-churched.

4. The quality and durability of a church's ministry is in large part determined by the strength of the organization evolved during the church's formative years, regardless of the form the church may take.

While succeeding chapters will support and build on these assumptions, a brief discussion of each point is appropriate here.

Societal Trends and the Need for New Churches

American society is dynamic. Old communities are changing, and new ones are continually being formed. Although the rate of population increase in the United States has slowed in the last decade, births continue to outnumber deaths, and in-migration from other areas of the world continues. Growth is taking place today in areas that did not grow during the last generation. In the 1950s population growth was concentrated in approximately one-half of the counties of the United States. Since 1960, 65 percent of the counties have gained population.

Areas of the country that were losing people a decade ago have now stabilized or are growing. This phenomenon can be seen especially in the South. After many years of population loss due to out-migration, the states of the Deep South are beginning to show a net increase. Fewer blacks are leaving the South, and significant numbers of blacks and retired people are moving from northern cities to the region. The increase of military installations and industrial complexes in the South has further boosted the number of people living there. The Upper Midwest, on the other hand, is experiencing significant population loss. Mobility continues in three basic respects:

1. Among communities—from city to suburb, city to rural areas, suburb back to the city, suburb to rural areas, rural to urban areas, rural areas to suburban areas, small town to city, city to small town, city to city, state to state, and region to region.

2. Among social classes—lower class to middle class, middle class to upper-middle class, rags to riches, riches to rags.

3. Among national and ethnic groups as they tend to move collectively from one community to another—A neighborhood that was first settled by German or Polish immigrants may later become populated by persons from the Appalachian mountain region. An area of Anglos may, after several generations, become predominantly Jewish, which may later become predominantly black, which may still later become predominantly Spanish. In Bridgeport, Connecticut, an Anglo community was later populated by eastern Europeans, then by blacks, and now by Puerto Ricans. In many cities what was originally an Anglo area later became black, but has today, again, become Anglo as redevelopment has occurred.

There has been major immigration of Asians to the United States during the last fifteen years—an 868 percent increase of Koreans (from 18,833 in 1960 to 182,392 in 1974), a 154 percent increase of Filipinos (from less than 200,000 to almost 500,000), and a 168 percent increase among Chinese (from 200,000 to 540,000). Rapid increase has also taken place in the Hispanic population of the United States. In-migration to parts of the Southwest and the Northeast has been particularly significant.

By 1985 it may be expected that one-half of the population of the United States will be living in the suburbs, whereas only 37 percent of the people in metropolitan areas now live outside central cities. One-fourth of the population will continue to live in central cities of metropolitan areas, and the remaining one-fourth will continue to live in rural areas. Perhaps one-third of the central cities will be populated by blacks and other ethnic groups compared to only one-fifth of the population today.

One of the interesting phenomena of the early 1970s has been the rapid reversal of a trend that saw most population growth during preceding decades in the suburban areas of the major metropolitan areas. Much of the population growth today and in the future is taking and will take place in smaller metropolitan areas as people have now begun to leave the larger metropolitan centers for more space. Of the two thousand nonmetropolitan counties that lost population between 1950 and 1960, 85 percent have begun to grow during the last decade. Most surprising is the movement back to small cities and towns that are located in nonmetropolitan areas.

By numbers of people, the big metropolitan areas continue to grow fastest, but between 1970 and 1973, metropolitan counties grew by only 2.2 percent while nonmetropolitan counties were growing by 4.1 percent. Most significant was the 3.7 percent growth rate in counties not adjacent to metropolitan areas; such growth could not be attributed solely to the mere expansion of a neighboring big city or its suburbs.

Other demographic changes are also taking place. For example, there is a sharp increase in the number of people in our society who live alone. Between 1969 and 1974, the average number of persons living in the American household fell from 3.19 to 2.97. Younger, middle-aged, and older people are choosing to live alone or with people who are not part of their own families.

Perhaps one of the most important changes for congregations is the growing number of young adults. The fastest growing age groups in the country now are those between twenty-five and thirty-four years of age, and the group between eighteen and twenty-four. While many of these people are staying single, or staying single longer, most of them marry and establish families by the time they reach their thirties. The large number of children who were born in the late forties and early fifties are now setting up their own households. This is happening at the rate of 175,000 per year in the age group under twenty-five alone. And most of them are having children, although not as many as in past generations. In fact, more first children were born in 1973 than in the peak year of population increase, which was 1961. There are, of course, significantly fewer second and third children born in families today.

An increasing number of retired people, many of whom are affluent, move to new communities at the time of retirement, particularly specially designed ones.

Finally, housing patterns in our society are changing. While most new construction continues to take place in the suburbs, it is of a different type than in the past. In the 1950s, most new homes were single-family homes. Today the number of townhouses and multifamily apartments and condominiums (spurred on by concern for energy and cost) is increasing. People who prefer their own single-family dwelling may be forced to consider the older residential areas of the cities.

The establishment of new communities does not depend upon rapid population growth alone, but on population mobility. As long as people are moving, new churches will be needed. Perhaps there has never been a time that was more right for their establishment than today.

Responsibility of the Denominations

Why do established denominations or judicatories[3] get involved in creating new churches in new communities? If

3. A *judicatory*, when used with reference to the Church, is a sub-unit of a denomination that encompasses a defined geographical area, the clergy and churches of the denomination within it, and is presided over by a person or group that has advisory, supervisory, and/or administrative power and responsibility. Some denominations have no intermediate levels between congregation and denomination; others have two or more judicatory levels. Some major denominations and their judicatories are: Baptist—association; Methodist—jurisdiction, conference, and district; Presbyterian—synod and presbytery; Lutheran—synod and district; Episcopal—diocese; United Church of Christ—conference and associa-

the church is indeed a primary social institution, one which must be present for the community to survive, why not let local people start their own? They best know their needs and the style of church that can best meet those needs. Perhaps more creative and relevant church growth would occur if local people were left to do it for themselves. The local people are the primary group in any church, but there are reasons why denominations do or should assist people in new communities to start new congregations:

1. There is a natural tendency for institutions to perpetuate themselves. No institution, including the church, can maintain itself indefinitely unless it opens new centers when it closes some older ones. For the church as a social institution, then, establishing new congregations becomes a matter of life and death.

2. Established denominations feel they have something to offer the residents of a new community; namely, the Christian gospel, financial backing, programmatic support, and experience in how to go about starting a church. Starting new churches is a method of evangelism, of reaching out to more people with the Christian message. The financial aid and expertise provided by the denomination allow it to carry out its evangelistic outreach in a community.

3. Residents of a new community, who are busy learning to live in their new environment, are eager for national organizations to help them create their basic organizations. Along with the practicality of having help, people in a new environment have a need, if not a hunger, for familiar institutions that can help them bridge their past lives with the present. Churches help to provide that stability.

As a community organization, then, the local church is first and foremost the creation and responsibility of local people. A new congregation cannot grow unless they parti-

---

tion. In those cases in which one person has primary responsibility for the denomination's ministry in a judicatory, he or she may be called moderator, president, pastor-at-large, superintendent, executive, director, or bishop.

cipate. It is established by and for them. There is a legitimate support function for the judicatory or denomination, however. They bring experience, expertise, financial backing, pastoral leadership, and relationships to churches in nearby communities.

Perhaps one of the most significant contributions of the denomination to the new church is the opportunity to be a part of the renewal and ministry of related congregations in declining neighborhoods of the larger area served. In the past we have divided church development concerns into redevelopment of existing churches and new church development. Perhaps this terminology encouraged the antagonism that has emerged between those who have primary concern with one or the other. The deteriorating, changing neighborhoods of inner cities need to be seen as opportunities for new church development just as the suburban areas, and the two thrusts need to be related. Is it not possible for us to increase our efforts in church extension[4] to the older residential areas as well as those areas where churches have not existed before? Is it not as important that the ministry of Old Trinity Church in San Angelo, Texas, located eight blocks from downtown in a community that is just beginning to change, be renewed or redeveloped as it is for a new congregation to be started in the upper-middle-class suburb where success is all but assured anyway? Would it be possible and advisable to yoke the inner-city church and newly developed suburban church into a parish from the very beginning in a way that would keep both congregations mindful of the larger context in which they both minister? This is now being done in Kansas City, Carrollton, Texas, and Texarkana, Arkansas-Texas. If it occurs elsewhere, it will be through the leading and challenging efforts of the denominations.

4. As used here, *church extension* and *new church development* are synonymous terms which denote the task or process of establishing new congregations. In other contexts these designations have been variously applied to the propagation of the faith through missions and evangelistic recruitment, the construction or renovation of church buildings, or experimentation with distinctive forms of congregations and styles of ministry.

New Opportunity

The creation of a new congregation, whether in the suburbs or inner city, is an opportunity for an established denomination to experiment with new forms of churches and to create models for other churches. The newly developed church is not bound to congregational traditions.

A developing congregation in the new town of Reston, Virginia, experimented with the best time to hold church school classes for children. They found that Tuesday afternoon was far better than Sunday morning. More children came on Tuesday, and they came with more regularity. This is now being tried in other churches that would not have made the change until the success of the experiment was verified elsewhere.

There is no reason why each new congregation should have to "reinvent the wheel." Past experiences are to be shared. But people can be challenged to try new structures and possibilities in those situations in which they are not tied to traditions established for them by preceding generations. There is no other time in a church's life when it is as free to create, innovate, and think about why it is there and why it is needed. It is a time to start over—a time to pray, to study, to search the Scriptures for Christ's purpose for the body which He called into being. It is an opportunity for people who have not been affiliated with a church before to begin a new life in an institution that will help to provide spiritual meaning and purpose for their existence.

The Early Years

Psychologists tell us that the first few weeks, months, and years of a child's life are the most important in terms of his or her future development as a happy and well-adjusted person. Pediatricians point out that strong bodies are built in the early months and years and that excessive deprivation at that time may lead to lifelong maladies. The experience of the past has shown us that the same is true of social and religious institutions and particularly of churches. Often, denominations rush to buy property, call a pastor, and organize a congregation in a matter of weeks. Little thought is given to proper timing, location, and the identity or form of the church. Where churches have been established with insufficient funds, with untrained leadership, in areas that could not support a new congregation, or in communities that needed another type of church, they have suffered throughout their existence. Many have not survived.

In a large area being developed in suburban Salt Lake City, the United Church of Christ started a new congregation too early and on the wrong side of the area. The United Methodists waited too long to organize a church there and could not find an adequate site they could afford. In Denver one denomination sold a prime new church site to help finance an ecumenical congregation that was poorly planned and located on a back street. The church has floundered.

Today, we have a framework and guidelines for the questions of when, where, and how in new church development. The congregations that use these guidelines are generally able to structure strong institutions that serve their communities well.

2 : Lessons from the Past

From the Forties to the Seventies

The character and quality of life within new communities and new churches has been of much interest and debate in recent years. Large areas of cities have been demolished and left vacant or redeveloped for a different group of people (often a higher income group). The poor have often been displaced with little attention given to their desires and welfare. In other places, new housing for the poor has been built in the form of high-rise ghettos, whereby thousands of indigent people are crowded into small land areas, resulting in increased social disorganization. "Urban renewal," "model cities," and similar government programs were hailed as the saviors of the cities, but often were disappointments.

At the edges of the cities, suburban sprawl continues. There are retirement villages, leisure cities, and mobile home parks. Single-family dwellings, townhouses, and low-density and multifamily apartments and condominiums proliferate to shelter the middle- and upper-middle-class citizens who are dissatisfied with life in the city and can afford better. Although many of them will continue to be dependent upon those cities for jobs and services, the suburbs, they think, offer respite from urban problems and an opportunity to live in a neighborhood with people who have similar values and life-styles.

Another relatively recent trend in the United States has been for large developers to go into rural areas, oftentimes many miles from existing towns and cities, purchase large tracts of land, and plan or build new self-sufficient communities. These new towns are designed as places to live, work, shop, and play. They are billed as havens for young and old, rich and poor, away from the problems of the cities. Few, however, have attained the success anticipated. They, as suburban communities generally, have failed to achieve diversity by providing for the poor as well as the more affluent.

New churches have also come under scrutiny and criticism in the last decade. Few would deny that an evaluation of past methods and practices was overdue and that many of the criticisms have hit their mark. Across America during the two decades following World War II, American Protestant churches organized hundreds of new, mostly suburban, congregations. Few cities in America had less than three or four new churches organized during this period, and in many metropolitan areas a score or more were started. Some of these did not survive their first ten years. Some others are small, struggling institutions today with less than enough members to be fully programmed, self-supporting churches.

There are many reasons why these churches have encountered problems. Some would have become strong except for bad location, too much debt, being too dependent for support on the denomination, or poor ministerial leadership in the beginning. In other instances, denominational and judicatory officials got carried away with church extension fever and simply assisted communities to start too many churches or the wrong types. Where a church was inaugurated without a community large enough or of such character to support an institution of its type, survival was never possible. In other words, churches and communities were inappropriately matched.

While there is more truth to these charges than some of us believe or admit, they do not adequately reflect our past efforts. A vast majority of the new churches established during the period have thrived. Most of them are strong, self-supporting congregations that have grown more rapidly than the other churches of their denominations and have returned more money to the denominational benevolence programs then they received from them.

We recently traced the progress of 350 new United Methodist churches started between 1958 and 1961. By 1972 they had an average (median) membership of 315 members compared with 150 average members in the denomination as a whole. By the end of the survey period, a church in Iowa had 1003 members, a church in Kansas City had 1407 members, a church in Lexington, Kentucky, had 1630 members, and a church in Houston, Texas, had 3978 members. Only 28 (8 percent) had less than 100 members.

But survival was not the only test of the adequacy of new church efforts during this period. Billions of dollars were spent on buildings, some of which have been liabilities for the members through the years or have turned churches into mere debt-paying societies. In other cases, the various denominations have gone their own way and "done their own thing" regardless of the plans of other denominations. It is not uncommon to find communities today in which several denominations have developed churches independently, leaving them to compete or struggle together.

Finally, the new church development enterprise of the past generation must respond to the charge of racism. The indictment has been made that new churches have been started almost exclusively in new, white, middle- or upper-middle-class suburban communities where minorities and less-affluent whites cannot afford to move or would be excluded if they could. In most denominations, we have often failed to start new churches in redeveloped urban areas and minority communities. Hopefully, the next round will be different.

An Upswing in Religious Interest

Signs of the recent past and present point to an impending upswing in religious interest in America following a long decade of drought. The widespread movement into the fundamentalist sects by the youth, the turning by some to mystical religions, and the significant growth of the human potential movement signal a search for meaning on a wide scale. It is understandable that this search at first would take place outside the established denominations. The "establishment" is always a target during times of upheaval. If the patterns of history are repeated, however, the concern for religion and meaning will move back into the established churches as the "sect groups" will not be able to provide the depth that is demanded, or the sects themselves will become established churches.

Two primary questions face established denominations today:

1. Will we be properly equipped to assist those who search for religious meaning as they increasingly turn to us?

2. Will we have congregations strategically located in new communities, as well as in older ones, to receive the "searchers" as they come?

The two questions are not unrelated. Those who participate in starting new churches must do more than provide buildings or social organizations that are called churches. The congregations must be equipped theologically and emotionally to deal with the demands that will be made upon them.

The return to the churches has already begun. There has been a de-emphasis on new church development in the last decade. It all but stopped in many areas of the United States and in several mainline Protestant churches. The need for new churches has accumulated, however, and American Protestantism is now venturing forth on a new wave of church extension. Churches in all parts of the nation are reporting the return of significant numbers of young people, young married couples, and middle-aged people back into the church. At the same time local congregations and judicatories are planning new congregations, buying sites, recruiting pastors, and conducting feasibility studies. During one month in mid-1975, I received fifteen inquiries regarding these aspects of new church development. That is more than were received in an entire year prior to 1974. Other church development specialists report similar experiences. Letters and calls came in that month from five denominations in nine states (Alabama, Florida, Maryland, Kansas, Missouri, Texas, Nebraska, Illinois, and Colorado).

Will the fresh round of new church development be appropriate for the next generation, or will it copy with only minor modifications the practices of the past? Some of the past methods and development techniques were adequate for that time. But in a society that some are calling postindustrial, post-Christian, and postaffluent, and one in which lack of energy, shortages, zero population growth, and new family life-styles may cause significant changes in the way people live, the characteristics of the church that can best meet people's needs for a religious fellowship must be rethought. The questions will have to be answered in a three-way tension between the purpose of the church, the experience of the church with new church development efforts in the past, and the new environment in which the church will operate in the remaining years of the seventies and succeeding decades.

Effective New Congregations

The characteristics of today's strong and effective new congregations that will continue to be important in the years ahead are difficult to define. Attributes considered necessary for congregations in certain kinds of communities, or for particular types of churches, may be inappropriate for others. But based upon our learnings from the past, we may hypothesize that the following general characteristics will be found in the most effective congregations:

1. The church of tomorrow will have balance. That balance will be evident in the amount of resources expended upon institutional maintenance and upon outreach in ministry. It will be found in the breadth of programming, both in terms of what is offered and who it is for—members, prospective members, and others. It will be expressed in the budget of the church, in the proportions designated for operating expenses, salaries, benevolences, and buildings.

2. The church will be marked by intentionality. The congregation will not let itself drift into premature traditions or become involved in activities because "a church is supposed to do them." Its purpose as a religious community will be intentionally sought and nurtured, and the leaders will be careful that all activities contribute to the primary task.

3. The congregation will be an open system. It will not only be open to all members of the community, but it will understand the community that it exists to serve and adjust its program as changes in the environment require it.

4. From the beginning the church will inaugurate and operate through a planning process that includes goals, objectives, strategies, and procedures that can be evaluated in terms of its purpose as a religious community and its strength as a social organization. The process will be an ongoing one in which new goals are set each year as former goals are attained.

5. The strong church of tomorrow will be led by a pastor who has been effective in his or her earlier ministry and is challenged by the opportunities presented by a new congregation. The pastor will also be a person who brings stability to the congregation instead of relying upon it for strength.

6. In a new church the membership may be small for the first year or so. Leaders, however, will be carefully chosen and trained for their tasks. They will be chosen on

the basis of their religious commitment and concern for the community, as well as their knowledge of finances, building, or administration.

7. Recruitment of members and solicitation of ministry opportunities will be important to the effective church in its early years, but these tasks will be carried out at a pace that allows for thorough and effective assimilation into the congregation. The church will be one in which all members have a part and a stake in its success.

8. As the church grows and develops, opportunities for education, service, and caring will be afforded through small groups. The church will offer a wide range of activities for the religious needs of its people, but in units of such size that intimacy and personal growth may occur.

9. The church will have a clear image of itself, which manifests itself in an intelligible image in its community. As a group, the church will know what it is about, and each member will be able to express and defend it.

10. The structure that houses the congregation's activities will represent the character and quality of members' lives together. When worship is desired, the building will facilitate it. When it is used for education, recreation, or service projects, the appropriate environment can be created.

11. In a literal sense, the new church of tomorrow will be a living room, a center in the community where people can find support, affirmation, redemption, and compassion.

12. The educational program of the church will be purposeful—an aid in the development process by which participants are sent back into the "world" to operate with strength and confidence.

13. While the pastor will represent and "symbolize" the gathered fellowship in much of its life, and direct many of its activities, leadership will be shared with the laity in tomorrow's church.

14. The effective church will allow individual members to talk about and nourish their own religious pilgrimage, finding strength and sustenance for their personal reli-

gious needs even as they participate in and contribute to the common life of all.

15. The church with the strength to face the future will be one which can incorporate within its life the elements of surprise, excitement, and expectation. Programs and activities that become "chores" will be questioned and eliminated. Unless joy can be expected from any event, even administrative ones, that event will not be held.

16. The church will seek opportunities for shared service with other churches in the community, whether they be of the same denomination or different ones. Jealousy, threat, and competition with other churches will not be possible as the congregation understands the larger ministry that all of them are about.

17. The church of tomorrow will be just that—one whose focus is on present and future opportunities, one that never allows "we have always done it this way" to go unchallenged.

Mistakes to Avoid

As past experience has enlightened church developers today regarding characteristics that are desirable in a church, we can also learn from the mistakes of our predecessors. Many of the traits and methods we will want to avoid in the development of new congregations have already been tried. The following are some major learnings from which the church of the next generation can profit:

1. When the decision is made to begin a new church, denominational, judicatory, and local community people have "high hopes." There is frequently anticipation that the new church will be one of the largest and "best" ever. The model is often the large metropolitan-regional church that was started some years earlier in another part of the metropolis or judicatory and is thought to be "very successful." It is important that the developers of a new congregation realize that few churches grow as rapidly. A church organized on Florida's gulf coast in 1974 had two hundred

members by the end of the first year. Most churches will do well to have one hundred people in that length of time. Recognizing the scope of the community that the church is meant to serve, the character of that community and the limitations and opportunities imposed by it, will issue in realistic and attainable goals. Failure to set goals that are within reach may lead to frustration and ultimately have a negative impact upon growth.

2. Some denominational executives have been concerned solely with "institutional success"—growing membership and achievement of self-support. The evaluation criteria in such cases are quantitative. Where the pastor and membership of a new church are responsible to their sponsors for this kind of success alone, with no thought for the quality of the religious fellowship formed, the church may be unable to function effectively no matter how hard it tries.

3. Several judicatories in the 1960s decided that ecumenical new church development was the wave of the future, and some completely stopped organizing new denominational congregations. In most cases the results have been tragic. A church, as any organization, needs a clear identity. Whether one supports the existence of denominations or not, they are realities in our society, and brand names do tell prospective members something about what can be expected in a church. To be vague in its identification, which is generally the case in an ecumenical church, whether intentionally or not, means that many people will not consider it. They reject it because they do not know what it is. A congregation clearly marked Presbyterian, for example, may attract more Lutherans and Methodists than one labeled Community or Interdenominational.

4. One of the most common errors made is locating a new church too close to existing churches of the same denomination. Examples abound in Corpus Christi, Madison, Columbus, Seattle, Albuquerque, and other medium-sized and large cities. In each of these cities there is at least one congregation of a mainline Protestant denomination that is caught in a frustrating struggle for survival because of

its location in the shadow of nearby churches of its denomination. Inevitably this leads to competition and hard feelings.

5. Many churches try to move too rapidly through the early development stage. Worship services are sometimes inaugurated the week after the pastor arrives. Similarly, educational classes and women's, men's, couple's, and youth groups are started during the early weeks. A new congregation should not expect to have a fully programmed and organized institution for several years. Before any new program is added, there must be adequate time for consideration of purpose and planning.

Forms of New Congregations

We have not always been clear and intentional in the past about the form of the congregation to be started in a community. Where clarity has been lacking, the judicatory, the pastor, and the members of the new church have worked toward different goals, and all have been frustrated. In the future, the form of the new congregation must be explicitly defined in the preliminary mission design prepared by the judicatory and accepted or redefined by the congregation in the final design. (see chapter 8).

Some variables are: How quickly, if ever, is the congregation expected to become self-supporting? What will be the predominant racial or ethnic group served by the new congregation? Will the congregation have a delimited focus and narrow appeal, or will it have a diverse program and recruit generally from its community? Will the new church be denominational, nondenominational, or ecumenical? Will the new congregation be located in a redeveloped urban area, suburb, small town, or new town?

The goals and methods of new congregations during the early years will differ. What may be appropriate for one form of new church may not be for others. There are basically six forms. We will define them here and refer to them in chapters 5 through 12 as the process of development is discussed in more detail.

FORM 1—"MISSION" CONGREGATION

Although some denominations use the term *mission church* for any new congregation, it is used here to designate a congregation organized to serve a community that for some reason cannot support a fully programmed, self-supporting ministry. The denomination or judicatory will recognize this fact in the beginning and not force success criteria on a church that has no chance of meeting them. In essence, the presbytery, diocese, district, or judicatory decides that there are people in an area who need a church and can or will have it only if the denomination organizes and supports it.

There are few intentional mission congregations in existence today, and it may be anticipated that they will be rare in the future. But it is one viable form. Frequently, churches that were expected to be self-supporting are not and become mission congregations through default. Such a church should be seen as a failure of another form rather than viewed as a mission congregation.

FORM 2—MINORITY CONGREGATION

Neighborhoods in cities, suburbs, and new towns may be populated by members of racial, ethnic, or nationality groups. In the mainline denominations, we have often sought to recruit these people as participants in existing nearby white congregations. For the most part we have failed. Many denominations have realized in recent years that new congregations must be developed specifically for minorities as their numbers increase—particularly in the cities. The Southern Baptist Convention and United Presbyterian Church in the United States, among other denominations, have been in the forefront of such development. Some denominations are just getting started.

The Christian Church (Disciples of Christ), a denomination of one and one-half million members, started eight new black congregations in metropolitan areas in the last twenty years and six in rural areas since 1960. In the United Methodist Church, third largest Christian denomination in the nation, only eleven new churches have been established primarily for blacks in recent years. This does not include formerly white congregations that have been redeveloped for blacks. While this denomination has a better record with regard to Hispanics, Asians, and Indians, its efforts have not kept pace with demand. The population influx or mobility of these minority groups in the United States in the recent past and continuing into the present has been great. Mainline Protestantism has ministered to only a small fraction of these people in their new environments.

The paucity of our efforts in the past means that we lack experience in minority church development. With so few examples and experiments, we have only limited knowledge about how to do it.

Methods will be different for each group. Minorities cannot be classified together in new church development just as they cannot be in other areas of life. The patterns of church life for blacks are quite different from those for Asians, Mexican-Americans, Haitians, Samoans, or others. The culture, traditions, and needs of each group must be considered separately as new religious institutions are designed.

We are not suggesting that the denominations should attempt to design congregations *for* minorities, or even that we should assist them in the same way that we support congregations for white communities. The institutions in minority communities must be developed by indigenous people with support from the denominations or established churches, but without paternalism or interference.

FORM 3—STYLE-CENTERED CONGREGATION

A style-centered congregation builds a fellowship around a specific life-style or one particular characteristic of the church. The focus may be worship, service, or intimate sharing groups. A life-style-centered church might appeal primarily to the counterculture, the very wealthy, young singles, or homosexuals. There is a style-centered church for homosexuals in Toledo; one for jazz musicians in New York; one for those who want to breathe burning incense as they watch psychedelic designs and listen to fundamentalist preaching in Seattle; one built around human development concerns in San Francisco; and one for young singles, which meets monthly for celebrative worship, in Atlanta.

These congregations seldom become very large and often do not attain self-support. Financial support by denominations for these churches is usually justified on the basis of their value as models. Some have served that function well, particularly those which built their lives around house churches or small-group life. Some of these churches, however, have become style-centered congregations through the efforts of a strong organizing pastor who wanted to experiment, rather than as a result of intentional design by the supporting denomination. Where experiments have not been intentional, they have often failed.

FORM 4—THE NEW CONGREGATION
IN THE REDEVELOPED AREA

In many cities, deteriorating and slum housing has been removed and replaced by new, generally multifamily, dwellings. In many cases this renewal process took place over a period of several years. Churches were often closed or relocated to other residential areas during that time. It is, therefore, not uncommon to find new communities near the core of urban areas that have adequate housing but lack churches and some of the other primary social institutions.

While it is difficult to minister to residents of apartments and multifamily dwellings, experiments have shown that it is not impossible. Nevertheless, it is a very different situation than that experienced by new churches in communities primarily developed with single-family housing. New churches are needed in the inner-urban areas, and in redeveloped rural areas too, but the form appropriate for each community may be unique. Experimental new churches in redeveloped areas of Milwaukee, St. Louis, Dallas, and Cleveland may provide some general models. Mission congregations may be needed in these areas until more models are developed and tested.

FORM 5—TRADITIONAL SUBURBAN CONGREGATION

This is the local church that most people think about when the term *new church* is mentioned. It is generally located at the heart of a newly developing residential area of the city. It is expected to be self-supporting in a reasonable time (usually five to seven years), is family oriented, and its activities include the traditional programs of worship, education, outreach, and fellowship. It is the form of congregation that mainline denominations have had the most experience and success in developing, and more is known about how to organize it than any other. As long as suburban communities continue to be built at the perimeter of the metropolitan areas of this country, it will be the most common form of new congregation.

FORM 6—ECUMENICAL CONGREGATION

An ecumenical congregation is initiated, supported, or identified in some way with two or more denominations. We have already pointed to the tragic consequences of many new ecumenical congregations started in the last two decades. Most of those which have experienced problems were union congregations—those which actually have full standing in two or more denominations, but are identified with none.

A different model for ecumenical congregations—the reciprocal model—holds more promise than many previous ones. The model was developed several years ago in northern California and has most recently been used in Phoenix, Arizona, and Arlington, Texas. It is still experimental. The reciprocally organized congregation, by mutual agreement of the participating denominations, is identified with one denomination, which has sole responsibility for supervision and placement of the pastor. The church receives financial support, however, from two or more denominations in the critical early years. Those denominations which invest receive benevolence money from the congregation proportionately. Through this means the financial risk of starting a new congregation is spread among the denominations as is the "pay-off" of benevolence income. Perhaps the most important benefit of the reciprocal model is that competition among denominations to have the first congregation in an area is reduced or eliminated.

Interdenominational Cooperation

It may bother some readers that the basic process of new church development described herein is basically a denominational one and that ecumenical cooperation is referred to only in subsections of chapters. These people will maintain that denominations are artifacts out of history and are no longer needed. They will see the existence of two or more churches of different denominations serving the same residential community as inevitably causing unnecessary competition. The pastor of a new ecumenical congregation in New Jersey recently commented, "It is no longer necessary, if indeed it ever was, to plant four competing congregations at the crossroads of every village and town."[1]

It is true that new churches have been started in the past by denominations quite apart from the plans and strategies of other denominations. Such actions cannot be defended. This does not mean, however, that lack of cooperation in the past should result in all future congregations being interdenominational or union churches, or that competition is inevitable in every community served by two or more churches.

Competition between churches develops where more churches are present than are needed to serve a given area

1. "Mission Memo," *New World Outlook*, June, 1975, p. 6.

or a particular size population. It exists where churches see their main goal as getting new members rather than rendering a ministry to the total community. Where there are an adequate number of churches in a community and the congregations are more concerned about quality of ministry than growth in numbers, competition does not appear.

Attachment to denominations is not breaking down, as some are prone to say. Studies conducted in several cities throughout the United States have shown that denomination is the key factor in most people's decision about which church to join. The pastor, publicity, program, and location rate behind denomination in this regard. When a person considers attending a church in a new community, he is most likely to visit first the church of the denomination that he attended before moving. Because of differences in local congregations and local communities, some people will change to another denomination for a time in order to participate in a particular type of church or style of ministry, but most will continue to be conscious of their denominational heritage. Denominations represent traditions of religious commitment and meaning. To disregard the meaning behind denominational names is to ignore the strengths of the various traditions with disastrous results for the Church and the people. To overlook that tradition by establishing only union congregations would mean that fewer people in the population will participate.

To be specific, in most communities, *a congregation labeled as part of a mainline denomination will attract more people from other denominations than will an ecumenical, interdenominational, nondenominational, or community church.* An Episcopalian, for example, knows something about a Presbyterian church but is not sure what to expect in an ecumenical congregation. A grocery shopper, finding that a store is out of a regular brand of peas, generally switches to another well-known brand temporarily rather than to one that is unknown. People shopping for a church do the same.

Denominations, then, dare not operate in isolation. Goals and strategies for a particular area should be shared and discussed. It is also important that congregations serving the same community continue throughout their existence to share in ministries requiring the resources of more than one. In general, our experience has been that ecumenical cooperation in order to extend the ministries of local congregations is successful. Ecumenical cooperation to build up or maintain institutions generally fails.

3 : The Purpose of the Church and the Need for New Congregations

The Religious Quest

From time to time, during a child's early years, it begins to wonder about the world around it. It begins to question, to learn, to put what it learns in perspective.

Gradually, events in the child's life lead it to consciously question the meaning of its existence, and the relation between that and the meaning of other processes, events, and phenomena in the world. The child asks: Who am I? Why am I here? Who put me here? From where did I come? What will happen to me after I die? What is the purpose of life? What do I want to do with my life? What kind of person do I want to be? What is enduring in this world? What is the meaning of this existence that I did not create for myself but cannot escape?

These are questions of religion—of faith. They are questions that each person raises and continues to ask until acceptable explanations are found. For most people this questioning is an evolutionary process that is constantly repeated and never reaches a final conclusion.

Tribes, clans, families, and communities have wrestled with these questions through the ages. To answer them, they have developed frameworks in which to make sense out of life. The framework and its content is the group's religion. It is built upon as new experiences and revelations lead the group to alter or express its faith in new ways.

Most people work out a religious framework for their lives that is based upon the religion of their parents. Many never waver from it. Some accept the family religion for a time but later construct a different one. Some may try to ignore the religious questions, particularly if a conscious framework is not available from the parents, live for the moment, and order their lives on the basis of their own cumulative experience of the world. But this too is a religion in that it is an attempt to operate in a framework that makes sense of life and that provides a way to deal with ultimate concerns. Any fully developed religion includes a god who is considered ultimate and dependable, opportunities to venerate and receive benefits from the god, values, moral codes, goals, and methods for achieving the goals.

Although each person sets values and constructs his own religious framework, the significant role played by tradition in shaping that religion binds the person to others who also have inherited it and to the institution that nurtures it. Except as people with similar personal religious experience organize themselves together in religious fellowships,[1] the tradition is not maintained and developed. It becomes fractured and fragmented. It may die out.

The Christian Faith

Christianity is a religion in which people for two thousand years in every part of the world have found an acceptable way of understanding and ordering their feelings about ultimate concerns, of making sense of the world, of finding meaning for their lives, and of expressing faith and hope about life after death. In each age the church has to

1. A *fellowship* is defined here as a group of people voluntarily associated with and joined to one another by reason of their sharing a common religious faith. Use of the term *community* is reserved for the designation of people who share a common geographical area.

come to terms with the faith it has received and reinterpret it. It has to reexperience God as creator and sustainer of life revealed in Hebrew tradition, as just and loving Father revealed in the birth and life of Jesus Christ, as redeemer accomplished in Christ's death, and as continuing presence and comforter through the Holy Spirit. It has to study and interpret the Bible as the primary source of God's revelation and appropriate its teachings regarding the values of the sanctity of human life and love of neighbor. It has to establish goals concerning the seeking of righteousness, working for justice, living in favor with God and neighbor, and sharing the faith with others. And it has to institute activities of worship, prayer, observance of sacraments, and obedience in daily life to achieve its goals.

The Christian Church

The Christian Church is the mystical body of people in all ages and in all denominations who have accepted, practiced, and found meaning for their lives in Christianity. The congregation is the primary unit of the Church. People are related to God in local churches in local communities, through fellowships of people who are like-minded in religious faith and who have accepted Jesus Christ as Lord and Savior. There, believers covenant together to participate in events that recall and manifest their common hope, to hear and gather sustenance from their common tradition, to strengthen the tradition through the common exploration of the meaning of life and their part in it, to participate in rites that celebrate the benevolence and assistance of their God, to share their faith with their neighbors, to prepare for their servant role in the community, and to be energized to operate in the world with purpose and strength.

It is primarily at the level of the local church that the *logos* is incarnate—the Word becomes flesh—that the Christian faith becomes manifest and operative in the lives of people and society. From the local church, Christians move out to the structures of society. In daily routines of work, school, recreation, travel, relaxation, family life, and sundry activities, the disciples of Christ witness to their faith, exemplify the values that emanate from biblical teachings, and lobby for, support, and participate in activities that promote righteousness, justice, and equality of opportunity for all people to find meaning and fulfillment of life. For Christians, meaning is found in life as it is facilitated for others.

As the faithful go about their lives in the assurance that life is meaningful and that they have a contribution to make to the world, there are times when they go aside into the church. The church must understand the concerns that brought them there, their expressed and unexpressed needs, and how it can facilitate their relating those concerns to God.

Some go weekly out of habit or to relate to people; others to find emotional release or to be stimulated intellectually. Some go occasionally for any one or more of many reasons. Some go as the cares and stresses of life lead to weakness or emotional upset. A crisis may issue in the inability to operate effectively. Life becomes fractured and purposeless. Whatever the reason, at these times Christians turn to the religious fellowship, the community of the redeemed, where they can express their dependence upon and receive new meaning and strength from the one who is absolutely dependable—the God revealed in Jesus Christ. When the church is fulfilling its primary task in the community at worship, mutually supported by people who share the same faith, lives are renewed. They incorporate that upon which they are dependent, God revealed in the Holy Spirit, into their own inner beings in order to move back into society as new beings. As they have moved into the church temporarily, they have been strengthened, rehabilitated, trained, and charged so that they may now not only find meaning in life, but give meaning to life in societal involvements. Periodically they return to the church. The process of oscillation from society to the church and back to the world continues.

To accomplish its purpose the local church is established as a social institution, a visibly present organization in the community that has relative permanence. It develops schedules of worship services and activities, a place for meeting, a budget to pay for its activities, and a professional clergy to lead and coordinate them. All of it is to enable the church to perform its fundamental purpose of correlating God's answers and people's needs.

The purpose of the church is realized as it knows and understands the dynamics of the community and concerns of the people whom it has the responsibility to serve, plans its ministry to facilitate the renewal and rebuilding of their lives when they are not able to live them with meaning and fulfillment, and performs that ministry efficiently and continuously. The church fails to fulfill its purpose when it assumes that the context in which it ministers is the same in every place, that the channels of effecting its ministry are eternally valid, or when it does not adequately understand its constituency and the distinctive methods necessary for serving them. It fails when it loses sight of its primary task, alters it to conform to societal trends, or substitutes a subsidiary concern for it. The church fails when it does not perform its task effectively and completely and the corporate and social nature of the Christian faith is not manifest in the community through the lives of its members.

Crucial Questions for the Next Decade

We have seen that the congregation is essential for the person who has accepted the Christian faith. When such a person moves to a community that does not have Christian congregations, or ones that are acceptable, he or she is left without the one institution that supports and gives meaning to life. As people move into new geographical areas, therefore, they need new congregations for people with common religious commitments.

We have also observed that congregations exist for four reasons:

1. *Koinonia*—to nurture a community of people with

shared religious faith as they recall and express that faith and return periodically in dependence upon God for renewal.

2. *Didache*—to develop and nurture the religious tradition that they have received and to pass it on to succeeding generations.

3. *Kerygma*—to be a base for sharing the faith with outsiders.

4. *Diakonia*—to prepare members for service in the world.

As we turn our attention in the next decade to the task of developing congregations in new communities, we must recognize the points at which congregations of the past have lost sight of these tasks or failed to carry them out effectively. The development of each new congregation must become an opportunity for renewal in each generation.

Whether the Christian Church as it is embodied in local congregations today can still provide meaning to life is a crucial question. Are local churches places where people can work out and develop values, find the center of their lives, and gain strength for operating in the world? Can these congregations function as meaningful centers for the larger geographical neighborhood? Is it possible that mainline denominations have become so large, powerful, and wealthy that the unique purpose of the congregation has dropped from view and preoccupation with maintaining the power of the social institution, hence the status quo, has become uppermost?

On the other hand, we must ask whether congregations that have lost their reason for being have responded to the accompanying guilt by engaging in activities that could be performed better by other social institutions or groups. If it is found that this is the case, new congregations must serve as renewal points that challenge and stimulate older congregations and the Church generally. Unless we use this opportunity for renewal, more social institutions will be developed that are only concerned with maintaining themselves or with performing functions for which they are not suited and that they cannot do well.

To say that we have enough congregations today, as some say, is nonsense. That assumes that growth and change will not occur. It is to be expected that people will leave one geographical area for others. Older congregations will decline, and new ones will be needed to continue to nurture and support the members.

It's true that we have too many church buildings in certain neighborhoods. But even though we have too many in one place, we do not have enough in others, and we will have to provide new ones.

What is needed today are congregations that understand their unique purpose as a Church and concentrate on fulfilling that function. We also need congregations that bring people together in strong social institutions. A congregation walks a tight line between falling into traps on either side: On the one hand, defining the congregation so narrowly as a religious fellowship that it cannot fulfill its larger function as a social institution; and on the other hand, defining its purpose so broadly that it forgets its primary task and becomes only a social organization dabbling in concerns best taken up by other societal groups.

4 : Principles of Congregational Development

The creation of a new church provides a time for renewal and experimentation, not only for the new congregation, but for existing congregations as well. The beginning of a new church is a time to rethink the theological purpose of the church, its relationship to the community, the historical tradition to be carried on in it, and the primary need for people to meet God there.

New churches are started, however, by people whose idea of a congregation has been molded to a large extent by the churches of which they have been a part or have known about. It is inevitable, therefore, that newly developed congregations will resemble present ones in many respects.

This is both unavoidable and desirable. It is important that we do not ignore the significant contributions of congregations through the centuries and fail to profit from past wisdom. Experiences of the past are to be built upon to construct more adequate institutions for today. To completely ignore the past is to repeat needless mistakes, to cut off new churches from the tradition that has given them birth, to make it impossible to feed back learnings from new churches for the renewal of existing ones, and to gather data, construct theories, and draw conclusions already available. The creators of new churches will want to question the assumptions and methods used before to build on the strengths that are found and to find ways of overcoming weaknesses.

As social scientists have studied congregations, they have developed principles and theories that are important for new church developers. A congregation interrelates with its community in predictable ways. As we are aware of some of the most common associations and relationships, we are better able to establish effective new institutions.

Types of Churches

In a city, metropolitan area, county, or judicatory, there may be ten, twenty, fifty, one hundred, or more congregations of a denomination. They differ in many ways. Some are small; others are large. Some are attended primarily by whites, others are made up of other racial or ethnic groups. Some have their own buildings; others meet in rented or shared space. Some have full-time pastors; others may be served by part-time clergy. Some have little activity during the week other than worship and church school on Sunday; others have full programs six or seven days each week. Some serve persons and communities of the lower socioeconomic classes; others serve middle- and upper-class communities.

The character of a particular congregation may change over time. Because of the key role of pastoral leadership in a congregation, a church may be very different under one pastor than under another. Congregations may also take on new characteristics as lay people come and go or as the communities around them develop or change. How do the developers of a new congregation determine the kind of church needed from the scores of attributes to be considered?

In addition to theological reflection on the type of religious fellowship that it wants to be, a new church must recognize what is sociologically possible. It must understand how it will be different from other churches. It must know the basis upon which people choose a church and why. With this information the congregation can mold its image, organize and program effectively, and respond appropriately to the nature of its community. The denomination or judicatory can use the information to develop a master strategy for serving the city or geographical area.

We must have a basis for differentiating types of churches. The following factors are key criteria:

1. Location of the church—Where a church is located with regard to residential, commercial, and industrial zones can affect both the make-up of its constituency and the style of its ministry.

2. Image—Any social institution has an image in the community. It is formed by the total impact of its building, leaders, members, program, and purpose. The image that is current may or may not accurately reflect the institution as it really is or as it perceives itself. A church with a certain image will attract people who desire that type of church.

3. New members—Some churches secure new members from a localized area, while others attract members from a large area—sometimes all of a major metropolitan area. Significant variations characterize congregations according to the breadth of geographical distribution of their membership.

4. Concept of community—People living on the same street, or the same block, may think differently about the limits of "their community." One may think of it as the few blocks that make up the residential area in which he or she lives. Another person may consider his community to be a larger area of the city, which is made up of several neighborhoods. Someone else may think of it as the entire city or metropolitan area. How a person conceives his community will affect his decision of which church to attend.

5. Social ties—Some people choose a church because

they know some of the members or have long-standing family connections with it. Even though they may have moved to another community, the attachment may be sufficiently strong to attract them to the church.

6. Size—It is not unusual to find people who prefer a congregation that is small enough for them to know everyone. Others desire a large institution which offers more activities and a wider range of programs.

While church members may not be conscious of all the reasons they prefer a certain church, the distinctions outlined above generally apply in church selection. A typology of local congregations based on these criteria gives six distinct types:

TYPE I—OLD FIRST CHURCH DOWNTOWN

"Old First" church is found in the central business district of the city—the area of governmental offices, commerce, and retail shopping. It is generally the oldest part of the city, and the church located there was probably the first one of the denomination in the area (hence, the name "Old First"). As the city developed, this church became quite large and probably helped to organize other churches of the denomination in the city.

During its peak years, which may have preceded World War II or occurred soon after it, the downtown church had the largest membership and the largest and best building of any church of its denomination in the city. It was the place where the city fathers and the elite of the city worshiped, although it probably covered a wider social and economic spectrum of people than any other church. It had the best church school and the most diversified program of activities. It was the church that hosted denominational meetings and contributed the largest sums to denominational programs.

The downtown central business district is the only geographical area in the city that may be considered neutral. All residents think of downtown as being part of their community, even if they basically consider their community as the local residential area where they live. When they go downtown to work, shop, or be entertained, they feel that they are still on their own "turf." The downtown church, therefore, is the one church in the city that can reach out to all residential areas to attract new members. Its membership is one of the most diverse. Its community is the entire city and, in some cases, the metropolitan area.[1]

1. See Ezra Earl Jones and Robert L. Wilson, *What's Ahead For Old First Church.* (The Selected Bibliography gives additional publication information on this and other primary sources.)

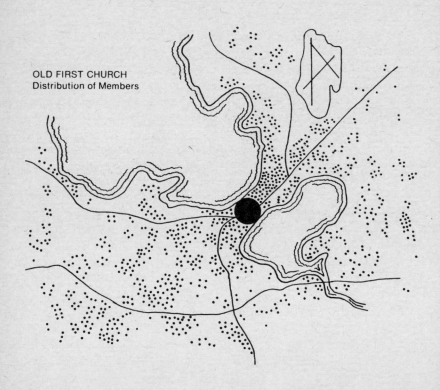

OLD FIRST CHURCH
Distribution of Members

TYPE II NEIGHBORHOOD CHURCH

One or more churches of a denomination may be located in a residential neighborhood of the city or suburbs. It is identified with and in large part affected by conditions in the community around it. It attracts most of its new members from the immediate neighborhood; thus, when the community has been fully developed, it has difficulty increasing in size. The church will grow while the local neighborhood is growing, become stable when it is fully developed, and decline as the neighborhood deteriorates. After many years of existence, its members may have moved to other parts of the city. Many, however, continue to come back to their former neighborhood for church

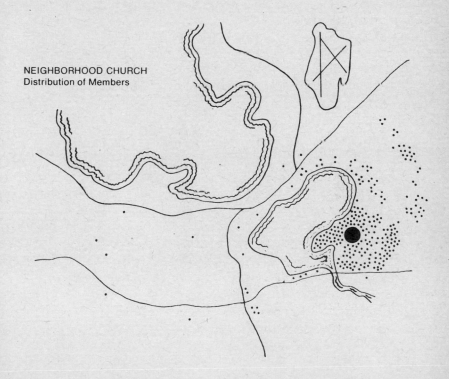

NEIGHBORHOOD CHURCH
Distribution of Members

activities. This does not mean that a neighborhood church can attract new members in significant numbers from other parts of the city; it rarely can.

TYPE III—METROPOLITAN-REGIONAL CHURCH

The metropolitan-regional church is located strategically at the growing edge of a metropolitan area, either within the city limits or in a suburb. It is highly visible and accessible to a number of residential neighborhoods in an area that is developing with middle- to upper-middle-class housing. This church is established at the "right" place at the "right" time. It is usually found on a major thoroughfare or at the intersection of two primary traffic arteries that connect a large section of the city to the main

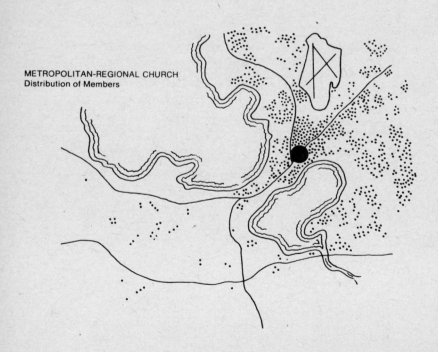

METROPOLITAN-REGIONAL CHURCH
Distribution of Members

shopping and business center. Rarely can a church that is hidden on a side street in one neighborhood or subdivision be a metropolitan-regional congregation.

These churches generally grow very rapidly and become quite large. There may be one or more older churches of this type in the city and a new one now developing. In some cases they take on the characteristics formerly attributed to the downtown church—large, beautiful building, noted pastor, wealth, and status. While this type of church does not draw from the whole city, it does draw new members from a large section of the city, particularly the "side of town" in which it is located, and that is its community.

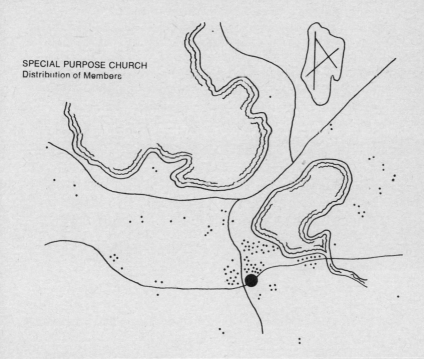

SPECIAL PURPOSE CHURCH
Distribution of Members

TYPE IV—SPECIAL PURPOSE CHURCH

The special purpose congregation, such as a church that structures its program around one issue or style of ministry, a church in which a language other than English is used, or one which has an extreme theological emphasis or unique charismatic leader does not attract the average churchgoer. Because it attracts people who want the unique kind of ministry that it has to offer, it may be located almost anywhere. People come to it because of its distinctiveness. The unique character of the church may cause it to become very large or to remain very small. Its community is the people who participate rather than a defined geographical territory.

TYPE V—SMALL TOWN CHURCH

Located in a town of a few hundred to thirty thousand or more residents, the small town church is the only church of its denomination in the community or town. It has many similarities to the downtown church in that it is generally located in the commercial core of the town and serves a diverse constituency. It is similar to the neighborhood church insofar as the small town itself may be thought of as a neighborhood. People living several miles from the town may drive past other churches to come to this church because of its centrality. Once another church of the same denomination is started in the town, the other types discussed above apply. Or as a metropolitan area grows, the small town may become a suburban community, and the church changes to a neighborhood or metropolitan-regional church.

TYPE VI—OPEN COUNTRY CHURCH

The open country church is found on a rural highway or secondary road in the open country. It serves a sparsely settled rural area, but also people who have moved into a nearby city or small town and prefer to return to the "old home church" for worship and other church activities.

These churches are usually small and may share a pastor with one or more other churches. Programming in the open country church usually consists primarily of worship, church school, and an occasional special activity.

CHURCHES IN TRANSITION

Most congregations fit one of these six categories. Some churches, however, due to community changes may be in flux at a particular time between one type and another. We have already seen the transformation that may take place in a small town church. In addition a downtown, neighborhood, or metropolitan-regional congregation may become a special purpose church or vice-versa. An open

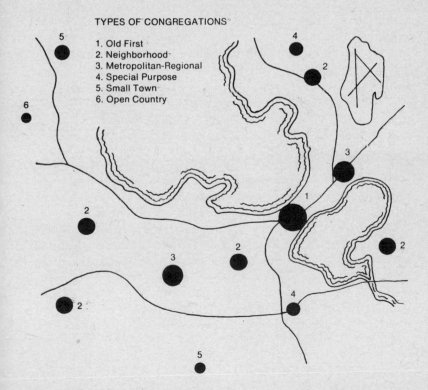

TYPES OF CONGREGATIONS

1. Old First
2. Neighborhood
3. Metropolitan-Regional
4. Special Purpose
5. Small Town
6. Open Country

country church may become a small town or suburban neighborhood church as community growth occurs.

The forms of new congregations discussed in chapter 2 (mission, minority, style-centered, redeveloped community church, suburban, and ecumenical) may fit any of these types for the most part. New church developers, therefore, must define the community to be served, determine the type of church to be created, decide the appropriate form for it, and proceed accordingly.

Each type has special opportunities and limitations. If property is purchased at the center of a subdivision, for example, the new congregation may not be able to attract people who live outside the limited neighborhood. If the church is located on a major thoroughfare, even at the edge of that community, it may be able to serve a much larger area and perhaps develop as a metropolitan-regional rather than a neighborhood church. If a special purpose church is desired, access is more important than location, but the number of people in the city or geographical area who want that unique type of congregation may be limited. Failure to recognize that churches differ and serve different communities may lead to the creation of institutions that cannot succeed.

Life Cycles and Organizational Growth

At the time a new organization or social institution is created, it is often possible and helpful to envision the patterns and cyles of its life existence. When a child is born, parents can forecast that, barring dramatic and unforseen circumstances, the child will grow rapidly during its early years, reach a plateau, and grow rapidly again during early adolescence. By the time the person reaches the late teens or early twenties, mature growth will have been achieved. Normally, the body will function with stability over several decades before illness or old age causes deterioration and eventual death.

An organization also has a life cycle. It, too, grows rapidly during the early years, levels off at certain stages, and perhaps grows further until maximum growth is achieved. It may then be expected to go through an extended period of stability before environmental changes or old age causes decline to the time of death. Death is not inevitable for organizations, though. Sometimes adjustments or changes within the organization allow it to continue in relative stability indefinitely or to reverse its decline before death occurs.

In the ideal situation, an organization, such as a congregation, builds a strong institutional base during its early years so that when it reaches maximum growth, it has enough members and resources to make the contribution and carry out the function it was organized to perform. If full maturity is expected too early, a firm foundation may be sacrificed and the long-term contribution of the organization impaired.

Gordon L. Lippit and Warren H. Schmidt have devel-

LIFE CYCLE OF A CONGREGATION

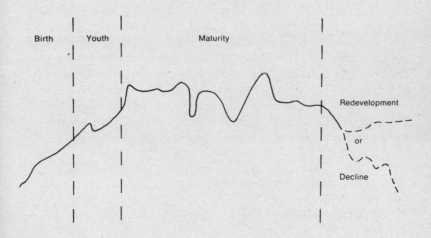

oped a pattern of the stages of organization growth.[2] As with persons, they see organizations going through the stages of birth, youth, and maturity. In birth, the critical concern is to create the new organization and help it survive as a viable system. In creating the new organization, the developers must be willing to risk failure. They can minimize the risk by drawing on past experience, but they dare not shy away from exploring untested areas. As they seek to help the organization survive, the creators must be willing to sacrifice early profits in order to fashion a viable system.[3] In the church, sacrificing early profits may mean delaying the start of activities, including worship, until the theological purpose and style of ministry is determined, and adequate resources are assured.

In the middle development stage of youth, the crucial task of the organization is to gain stability and a reputation and to develop pride (to fashion an image that is positive and attractive to the organization's members). The leaders must know how to organize for stability. At this point the issue "is whether management (clergy and lay leaders) can face up to the constant need to monitor, review, evaluate, and improve."[4]

Those organizations which are able to gain stability and build an image that reflects their primary task move to the level of maturity—the level sought by all organizations. At this stage the organization attempts to achieve uniqueness and adaptability. If it does, it can make its contribution to the community it was designed to serve. The key issue for the organization during its mature and productive years is whether it is receptive to changes in its environment that may necessitate adjustments or even drastic changes internally, and whether a degree of maturity has been attained

2. "Crisis in a Developing Organization," *Harvard Business Review*, November-December, 1967, p. 103. See also Gordon L. Lippitt, *Organizational Renewal*, p. 29.

3. Lippitt, *Organizational Renewal*, pp. 30-32.

4. *Ibid.*, p. 34.

that allows the organization to make its contribution to society without being preoccupied or overly concerned with its survival.[5]

The first five years of a new church's life are probably the most critical. During these years traditions are set, leaders are appointed and put to work, and a constituency is recruited that is large enough to make the operation viable. The church cannot afford the luxury during this period of postponing the primary task for which it has been created. But it also cannot become so concerned with "production" that critical mass is not achieved and problems of survival are extended into later years.

Creating a Setting

Every time a new church is organized, a new setting is created. Seymour B. Sarason points out that a setting is created anytime that "two or more people come together in new and sustained relationships to achieve certain goals."[6] Whether it is two people coming together in marriage or many people becoming involved in the organization of a new church, a new civic club, or a street gang, a new setting brings into existence a complex of involvements and interrelationships that are unique and potentially promising.

When a new setting is created, two things generally happen:

1. The establishment and organization of the new setting is patterned after ideas, ideals, and images in the minds of the people creating it, based upon their past experience with such groups. They assume that certain characteristics of the new group are automatic, that they have to be, that they are in the nature of new groups. Hence, certain assumptions about the new group are never tested. Sarason says that "the social context from which a new

5. *Ibid.*, pp. 35–38.
6. *The Creation of Settings and the Future Societies*, p. ix.

setting emerges, as well as the thinking of those who create new settings, reflects what seems 'natural' in the society. And what seems natural is almost always a function of the culture to a degree that usually renders us incapable of recognizing wherein we are prisoners of the culture. Those who create new settings always want to do something new, usually unaware that they are armed with, and will subsequently be disarmed by, categories of thought which help produce the conditions the new setting hopes to remedy."[7]

2. There is a tendency for the new organization to become a closed group, oblivious to the important ways in which the environment of the group impinges upon it and, on the other hand, how the group itself affects its social environment. "Those who create settings, including the far wider range of people than only system designers, have always overwhelmingly tended to proceed as if social realities were non-existent or so simply structured as to be of little account."[8]

In the creation of a new religious institution, the designers or developers assume that certain characteristics of churches have always been and will always be important. Therefore, they include traits without thinking about whether they are needed, and if needed, whether they should be modified.

Let us look at an example. In chapter 12, we present the proposition that a church needs a "place," a building where it can carry on its activities and from which it can send its people and program into the world. After giving it much thought, we believe the statement is valid for the church, particularly a new church. That statement shows, however, that we, as most people, have difficulty conceiving of a church apart from the building that houses it. It may just be that our concern to think about the building for the new organization keeps us from thinking about

7. *Ibid.*, p. xii.
8. *Ibid.*, p. 279.

what a new church can be apart from its physical accoutrements.

Sarason says, "When I assert that the tendency to put up new buildings to house new settings is frequently an invitation to disaster, it is not because I am in principle opposed to new buildings but because I want to demonstrate that the presumed need for new buildings can effectively obscure examination of issues and assumptions that argue against construction."[9] He goes on to say, "We know how to put up buildings, and that reinforces the thought that we should put them up."[10] In other words, when faced with a complex situation in which what-to-do-next is not easy to determine, we may attempt to get off the hook by doing the one thing that we know how to do—construct a building. On the other hand, we sometimes do things in creating new organizations or settings simply because we do not know how not to do them. To think creatively about a thing that we have some knowledge of is difficult.

There are other assumptions that new church developers take for granted, or assume are natural, as they develop new churches. These assumptions may or may not be valid, but they are commonly made and should be tested by any new congregation:

1. A new social institution must have a designated leader.

2. A church's schedule of services and activities should be primarily oriented around Sunday morning.

3. Mainline Protestant denominations are basically alike.

4. For relative permanence to be achieved in a church, a permanent membership roster with requirements for membership is imperative.

5. Most church people have or can be led to have concern for the poor and disadvantaged.

6. Worship consists of praise, confession, thanksgiving,

9. *Ibid.*, p. xii.
10. *Ibid.*, pp. 179–80.

preaching, and dedication (in that order), and for no longer than one hour at a time.

If new churches are to serve as opportunities for experimentation, model building, and the renewal of the whole church, we must do a better job in creating them. We must find ways to free ourselves in part from past assumptions. At the same time we cannot ignore the consequences of parting too radically from traditional patterns. The more different new congregations are from existing congregations, the less likely they are to be useful as models. We walk a thin line.

The Segmentation of Church Constituencies

At a recent church development conference a participant pointed out that "tremendous barriers are created by social class differences in the church as well as in other social organizations." The discussion that followed centered on the "rightness" and "wrongness" of the assertion. Very quickly the conferees, at least the vocal ones, reacted to the statement by supporting or rejecting it in what proved to be a very emotional discussion.

Those who objected to the statement were the idealists, people who wanted to believe that there are no artificial differences among people as they stand before God. They held that some churches successfully include all classes. These people pointed to the "wrongness" of social class barriers in the church and used the opportunity to lobby for openness.

Those supportive of the statement tended to be the realists. They were not advocating social class barriers in the church or any other organization. They were recognizing, however, that such barriers do exist and that they will not be eliminated in the church by some members wishing they were not there.

Christians support the assertion made by Paul that as people stand before God, "there is neither Jew nor Greek, there is neither slave nor free, there is neither male nor female" (Gal. 3:28, RSV). The commonality of people is symbolized in the sacrament of Holy Communion. Regardless of status or wealth, we all drink the same wine and partake of the same bread. Water and crackers are not given to some while wine and cake are given to others. It would be unthinkable to organize or plan programs in a church that would in any way support the continuation of the varying conditions of people.

If the commonality of mankind before God, however, blinds us to the differences that exists in society, the church will be guilty of irrelevance and disregard for social relations. The church must speak to people where they are—in wealth and in poverty, in strength and in weakness, in power and in powerlessness. We must not allow our concern for all people to blind us to differences in people that affect their church involvement and the kinds of church activities in which they participate. Recognizing the church's responsibility to all people, we can differentiate the people of a community for whom the church has responsibility but whom it serves in different ways.

One way of segmenting the population in the community served by a congregation is by current relationship to the church: (1) members, (2) prospective members, and (3) others.

Members have already committed themselves to the religious institution. They are to be served by the church and to offer themselves for service in it.

Prospective members are people in the community who may be open to participation as members in the church at this time in their lives. They may not have been open to it in the past. Some of these only need to be asked; others may come anyway. Some may need more incentive, including knowledge of what goes on in the church, before deciding.

The *others* are those who are not now in the church, may not be prospective members at this point in history, but who can be served by the church if it is concerned enough to find the appropriate means. This does not mean that the church can decide who they are, as opposed to prospective members, or that the church will not continue to work to include them in the fellowship. It does mean, however, that the church must recognize that at this time its primary ministry to these people may be through means other than inviting them to join.

Avery Dulles recently listed five models of the Church that he believes are necessary to understand its mystery.[11] He differentiates the models according to the manifestations of the Church in the world. After discussing the first two models of the Church, as Institution and Mystical Communion, which are the polar views from the most empirical to the most abstract, he discusses the Church as Sacrament, Herald, and Servant.

The Church as Sacrament brings together the human and divine in the congregation. This is the model of the church member. The church member is human. He sins, but through the Church finds redemption and forgiveness through meeting God there.

The Church as Herald is mediator of the Word of God to those who have not accepted the redemption offered by God and brought about in Christ, but who are fertile ground to hear and believe. This is the model with applicability for the prospective member.

Finally, the Church is not selfish. It offers itself, its resources, and the good news of redemption in Christ to all people, whether they now or ever will be members of the congregation. The model of the Church as Servant, if accepted, will not let a congregation become inward-looking and exclusive.

What responsibility does a congregation have to each of these three groups of people? How does it plan its ministry for each group? To fail to recognize that the needs of members may be different from those of prospective members or others outside the church may mean that the pro-

11. *Models of the Church.*

gramming is not intentional and has little impact upon and benefit for any of them. Perhaps churches would have fewer inactive members and could extend their ministry to many more people if they asked these questions periodically.

Further segmentation of a church's constituency is possible within each of the three categories just discussed. We shall discuss three methods:

1. Where congregations have differentiated their constituencies, they have most often done so on the basis of demographics. The church studies itself and appraises its community in terms of such characteristics as age, sex, social class, marital status, type of housing in which the people live, race and ethnicity, and parental state (whether adults have children and whether the children are still at home). If the community is found to consist of a large number of young adults, special programming for this group is planned. On the other hand, if a large number of singles of all ages are found, rather than programming primarily on the basis of age, the particular needs of singles of all ages become the basis of programming. Many churches already use this method of "knowing their people" even though it is not always done consciously and systematically.

2. A second method for differentiating the needs of the people whom a congregation has responsibility to serve is segmentation by life-style. The criterion used is the way people structure their lives, including how they use their leisure, how they dress, the kinds of activities in which they become involved, and the philosophy of life that underlies their actions. A church may find that the people in its community include all ages and types as described by demographics and that they are differentiated by the way they live their lives.

The community served by a particular congregation, for example, may be located near a recreational area. Many of the people may spend weekends including Sundays in recreational activities and do not participate in the congregation. They may want to participate in the church, but the congregation does not schedule and program appropriately for their life-style. Recognizing this fact, the church may find it necessary or advisable to schedule activities at other times of the week than Sunday morning.

3. Life situation, or situation of immediate need, is a third method of differentiating the constituency of a congregation. Knowing the demographic characteristics and life-styles of the people in the community, a congregation may find that people who vary significantly in these ways nevertheless have special needs in common at certain times. Perhaps there are people whose lives are dominated at a particular time by serious illness in the family. These people may have very different life-styles and demographic characteristics yet share a need for the supportive and healing ministry of the church. The church may be the one social institution that can bring them together in a mutually supportive fellowship.

One church on the West Coast found during an economic recession that there were a large number of unemployed people in its community. The condition affected male and female, young and old, people in higher income categories as well as in lower ones, people whose social life had been built around extended vacation trips as well as people who rarely ventured away from home. At this time in their lives they had a very important attribute in common—they were without a way of earning a living. The religious, psychological, and emotional effects of this condition meant that the church could have a special ministry to them that would not be possible at other times in their lives or for other people at this time. In addition to support groups for these people, the church was able to hire some of them temporarily to work for the church and to assist in finding jobs elsewhere.

Perhaps there are other ways of differentiating people in order to serve them in meaningful ways. What is important is that churches recognize the differences, understand them, and search for ways to respond. The assumption that a church only has to establish quality programs and advertise them to attract participants (even though some people may come) may mean denying the ministry of the church to other people who need special ministries or will respond if the programming is more flexible and diverse. The church's agenda is set by the needs of the people in its community. The church must structure itself appropriately to relate that agenda to the revelation and judgment of God.

Institutional Survival vs. Outreach in Ministry

Most mainline Protestant denominations have lost members each year since the mid-1960s. Much discussion has taken place around this issue, but the reasons for the loss are still in dispute.

One reason frequently given for the decline in numbers in established churches is the failure of mainline denominations over the last ten years to organize new congregations in new communities. Statistics which support this assertion are available. A study of the 488 new churches organized in the United Methodist Church during the three-year period, June 1958 to June 1961, reveals that these churches grew more rapidly than the average church in the denomination. In 1973 the 488 churches represented 0.9 percent of the churches of the denomination but 1.4 percent of the membership. If new churches had been formed at the same pace until now, and if they had grown at the same rate, this denomination would have suffered only minor losses.

But if the primary reason an organization opens new centers is to avoid loss or extend the organization, the goals are only survival ones, and the organization eventually dies for lack of purpose. In the church the purpose may be stated in religious terms although the activities of the group reveal other reasons for its existence. The congregation may emphasize recruitment of new members under the guise of evangelism. It may spend a significant

amount of time in fund-raising ventures and call it stewardship. It may concern itself with the construction of a building with no thought of how the building relates to the
religious goals of the congregation.

The group justifies its emphasis upon survival in the
early years by pointing to the necessity of building a
strong organization in order that its ministry may be maxi-
mized at the time the organization reaches maturity. But
one has to question whether a church that is not first and
foremost concerned with its primary religious task can
ever reach maturity. What force could cause it to turn away
from survival goals to the primary goal of relating people
to God if it never had that purpose?

A new congregation is organized for the purpose of being an "arena" in which the people of the community to
be served may come together in a supportive religious
fellowship to be renewed and recharged for living in and
contributing to society. Regardless of whether a local congregation chooses to express its purpose in these words, it
must begin its task at this point and spend adequate time
clarifying its reasons for being. It can then consider the
type of social organization that is needed to fulfill the purpose. The group must recognize that certain institutional
(survival) goals must get more attention in the early years,
but those efforts should be seen as means to an end. Not
only must each survival effort be appraised in terms of its
support of the religious goals, but the question must in
each instance be asked, Is there a possibility that this will
interfere with our primary goals? Concern with survival
may be more than wasted effort; it may stand in the way
of a group's thinking about its real purpose.

A study by Donald L. Metz in 1964 of six new congregations on the Pacific Coast found that survival goals are
much easier to define than formal goals (which he lists as
community [fellowship], nurture, and service).[12] He points
out that there is a tendency for a group to get on with what

12. *New Congregations.*

they agree upon and can do without conflict. Centering on survival tasks helps to unify the congregation. This overpowering desire to reduce conflict, to side-step those issues that are more complex, such as training of lay leaders, dealing with the insecurity of the ministers, or reacting to the expectations of the denominational agencies that initiated the new congregation, may set the church on a course of survival from which it can never recover.

Every congregation, new and old, must concern itself with both the purpose for which it is called into being and maintenance of the institution developed to support it. At certain times in its life, the church may need to give more attention to maintenance than at other times, and ministry may occur even as these goals are pursued. But at all times it must be aware that survival activities are means to serve the larger purpose of ministry. At no time in a church's life can it afford the luxury of seeing itself only as a religious community called out of the world. On the other hand, it cannot afford to succumb to the temptation of evaluating its success in terms of the growth of its membership, the size of its budget, or the beauty of its building.

PART II

The Process

5 : Developing a General Area Strategy

Responsibility

Responsibility for developing new congregations is lodged at different levels in the various denominations. In some denominations, particularly the smaller ones, it is placed with the denomination itself or with one of its general church agencies. Most mainline Protestant denominations develop new congregations through judicatories. Others create new congregations through existing local churches: a church recognizes the need for a new congregation in a neighboring area, sponsors it, and nurtures it until it is strong enough to continue on its own. In some judicatories new church development responsibility has been delegated to a church extension or church development committee, which raises money, buys sites, helps to organize the churches, and makes grants to the new congregations during the formative years.[1]

Regardless of responsibility, most church bodies allow a

1. Several denominations have prepared manuals to accompany this book that explain in detail the methods and procedures for developing new churches in those denominations. Write to your church development office for information about the availability of a manual for your denomination.

new church project to be initiated at any level. Even if the judicatory is responsible for starting churches, a local church may be first to sense a need and call attention to it. The local church may further participate in the initial study to see if a new church is justified.

Most judicatories or committees responsible for the process have a director or administrator who directs the developmental process and has primary responsibility for conducting a general area survey. This person is an important factor in the success of any new church development project. If he or she guides the process adequately, the steps are done on time and in the proper order. When this person does not accept the responsibility, a clear and logical process may not be carried through, and important tasks may go undone.

General Area Survey

A prerequisite of any new church development effort is a general survey of the geographical area in which a new church may be needed. This survey is a study of a judicatory, a county, a metropolitan area, or any clearly defined sociological or political unit. It may be drawn on political lines such as cities, counties, urbanized areas, or it may be an area that is delimited or partially so by primary barriers such as rivers, mountains, green belts, or large public areas. One recent survey in St. Louis included a three-county area. Another included the west side of Chicago and the western suburbs. Generally, the metropolitan area (Standard Metropolitan Statistical Area as defined by the Bureau of the Census)[2] is a logical unit for study. When one has not been defined, the area usually should include the entire town or city, the suburban fringe, and enough of the surrounding rural land so that future growth and expansion can be considered.

2. A city or cities of 50,000 or more population with adjoining urbanized counties.

The purpose of the survey is to obtain a comprehensive view of the area. It is an opportunity for a denomination to develop a total strategy. New church development will be one part of it, but it will be related to the continuing ministries of existing churches. The area strategy also enables existing local congregations to reappraise their environments so that they do not become closed systems. It allows a denomination to extend or reduce its ministry in an area on a sound basis.

The general area survey is one of the most opportune times for ecumenical cooperation in the whole developmental process. Each denomination should have its own committee and its own process, but much of the information needed by one denomination will be needed by all. It is wasted effort for each group to gather the same information separately. Representatives of the various denominations may discuss the descriptive data with each other in order to understand the different perspectives and opportunities. The analysis and interpretation for each denomination may be done separately and brought to a common meeting for sharing and adjustment in light of the plans of other groups. Ecumenical cooperation at judicatory levels generally facilitates cooperation at the local church level. Where it is missing at that level, it may be more difficult to implement in specific communities.[3]

Ideally, a general area survey should be conducted five to ten years before any new church development projects are needed. This will allow time for purchase of sites well before the communities in which they are to be located are developed and costs become exorbitant. It is becoming increasingly difficult, however, for denominations and judicatories to purchase good sites several years before they are needed. Finances are limited, and developers often

3. The leaflet, "Designing Today's Congregations—Guidelines for Cooperative Strategies," available from the Joint Strategy and Action Committee or denominational church development offices, is a helpful resource.

buy large tracts of land ahead of the churches and hold it. It is still the ideal, however, when and wherever possible. Following the first comprehensive area survey, a restudy should be conducted every three to five years in order to stay aware of changes in the community and to adjust plans as needed.

Sometimes the judicatory executive conducts the general area survey personally. Generally, however, a survey committee should be formed under his guidance to perform the vital function. The remainder of this chapter is addressed specially and personally to that committee.

Mapping the Survey Area

In the first step of the survey, a geographical and ecological study of the area should be made in order to determine its present land use. This will enable you to understand the form and boundaries of existing and potential residential areas. Secure several copies of a noncopyrighted map, one which can be reproduced without permission, from the local Chamber of Commerce, state highway department, or state or county planning commission. Put as much information as possible on one map, but do not put so much that it cannot be easily understood. The use of transparent overlays may be helpful when trying to comprehend large amounts of data.

As your next step, plot on the map the permanent or semipermanent features of the city which, in addition to serving other purposes, structure the community into differentiated parts:

1. Highways and transit lines—Begin by noting major transportation routes, such as railroads, waterways, highway thoroughfares, and mass transit right-of-ways. You are primarily interested in those highways and rail lines which create barriers between sections of the city and those which carry major traffic into, out of, or around the core city. Less important routes, which may be feeders

from residential communities into the major arteries, may be shown, but with less emphasis. Traffic counts can be secured that show traffic flow and the direction most people travel for various activities.

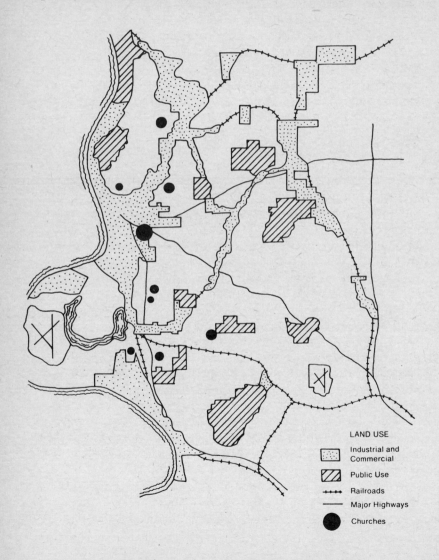

LAND USE

Industrial and Commercial

Public Use

Railroads

Major Highways

Churches

2. Commercial zones—Designate all major commercial tracts and shopping centers in the area in one color. Include the downtown central business district, which may have an exact definition (check with the planning commission), neighborhood shopping centers that have existed for many years and have a minimum of six or eight stores, strip-commercial zones along major or semimajor highways, new neighborhood shopping centers with one or more department stores and specialty shops but serving a limited area, and regional shopping centers with hundreds of stores, perhaps an enclosed mall, and covering hundreds of acres of land. Commercial zones serve as barriers, as do traffic arteries, between the various parts of the community, and help to shape the community into differentiated segments. They are also places to which all people go periodically for goods and services. The location of banks and other local financial institutions may give important information about primary commercial centers in the community. A study of traffic patterns between residential areas and significant shopping centers may reveal major streets upon which new churches can be located.

3. Industrial tracts—Show on the map those districts which are set aside for, or are now used for, heavy industry, manufacturing, and warehouses. These segments of the community are located primarily along rivers and railroad tracks, either near downtown or in industrial parks along major transportation arteries in the suburbs. Do not try to show every manufacturer in the city. Include only those that cover several blocks, act as barriers, or in some way help to shape the city.

4. Other primary barriers—With a different color marker, emphasize the tracts of property of nonresidential use that cover significant amounts of land and separate residential areas by impeding access from one community to another. Include waterways such as rivers, lakes, canals, marshes, and swamps; railroad right-of-ways; and mountains, steep cliffs, and ravines. Also, mark large public tracts that will

be perpetually nonresidential. Show reservoirs, large parks, cemeteries, golf courses, refuse areas, transportation right-of-ways that may not be used now as highways but that are designated for such and may be used in the future, extensive complexes of public buildings, large estates, campuses, large hospitals and institutions, and airports.

In urban areas where the planning commission has land-use maps, or maps projecting future land use, already drawn, the plotting of the above-listed features may be simply a matter of copying from one map to another. Where the information is not already available, "wind-shield" surveys, in which a person or committee drives through the community (taking one section at a time) and notes the various uses of the property, should be used to gather the information. When the four types of land use have been shown on a map, the sections of present and potential residential use will have begun to take shape. Using dotted or broken lines, outline the residential sectors. Some of the residential areas may be clearly marked on all sides by barriers. Others extend into open country with alternating areas of residences and open space that has not yet been developed. Do not close in these residential communities on all sides. The broken line will designate the developed part of the area; the open-ended side will show the possibility of future development. The map should now reveal those parts of the survey area that are open spaces and may be targeted for future housing developments.

On the same map or on a different map, differentiate the residential neighborhoods by the following means:

1. Using your own color or designation scheme, differentiate the residential communities by race or nationality. Where communities are mixed in this regard, show the predominant character of the community or have a special designation for those in transition.

2. On the same map or a different one, show population density in the residential sections. Again, some commun-

ities do not fit neatly into one category or the other, and a decision will have to be made by the mapmakers. Show neighborhoods that are composed primarily of single-family dwellings, townhouses, low-density apartments (three or four stories high or less), high-rise apartments, and

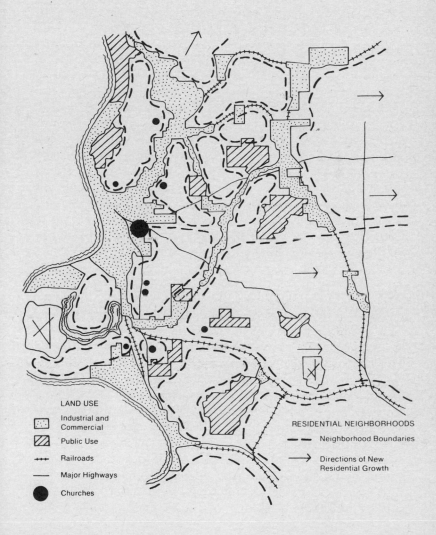

LAND USE

Industrial and Commercial

Public Use

+++ Railroads

— Major Highways

● Churches

RESIDENTIAL NEIGHBORHOODS

- - - Neighborhood Boundaries

→ Directions of New Residential Growth

mobile homes. The type of housing determines whether an adequate number of people are present in an area to support a new church, or whether they are likely to be people who normally attend church in significant numbers. A larger proportion of people living in single-family houses attend church than those living in multifamily dwellings. Density of population will be an important factor, then, in the location and development of a new church.

3. Note other social characteristics of the residential neighborhoods such as slums, localities in the beginning stages of deterioration, high-crime districts, parts of the community scheduled for destruction or renewal, and tracts that were cleared in the past and are still vacant. Each denomination should know which social classes of people it has served traditionally and which ones it has been unable to serve. This information should not be used to limit the denomination to serving certain people; it should be used to help it recognize (1) those communities in which a congregation may be developed into a strong social institution and (2) those to which it may want to extend its ministry with the recognition that self-supporting congregations may not be possible.

Other Considerations

There are other characteristics of the geographical area being surveyed that you should know about but that do not lend themselves to designation on a map. These may be summarized in the following categories:

1. Nuisances—Loud noise from industry and airports, smoke and pollution, or strong odors may make living undesirable in some neighborhoods. For example, a paper mill may cause offensive odors for certain parts of the city.

2. Unplanned development—Some localities may be undesirable because of past use or unplanned development that led to a mixture of junkyards, small unfinished and unattractive homes, nuisance industry, finer homes, and other sundry uses. It may be an unincorporated sec-

tion that developed in this manner before zoning laws went into effect and that will be slow to develop in the future. There may still be some areas that are not zoned.

3. Availability of utilities—Since most people in our society have easy access to telephone service, electricity, gas, water, and sewers, we assume that such utilities are readily available in any area or can be made available. This is not an accurate assumption and should be tested with regard to undeveloped sections. Telephones and electricity are generally available in the most remote areas, but not always. Many areas, however, are left undeveloped because water and sewers are not available. This may be due to topographical features. Sewer lines seldom cross over watersheds. Whereas planners in the past held that transportation arteries led development, they will tell you today that water lines and sewers are the most significant factors affecting when and how an area will develop.

A new church was organized in a western suburb of Milwaukee, Wisconsin, seven years ago with the expectation that the farmland around it would be developed with new homes. Today, few homes have been built, and significant development is not expected for another decade. The sole reason for the lack of development is the failure of the utility companies to extend water and sewage lines into the area.

4. Political considerations—Zoning laws, building codes, enforcement of building restrictions, and guidelines concerning subdivisions and new towns are subject to political decisions. The reason that sewer lines are extended into one area rather than another may be political. Churches that plan without taking political characteristics into consideration may find that they have overlooked one of the most important factors.

5. Economics—New residential communities develop as population increase occurs. One of the most significant determinants of population growth is the availability of employment. Employment opportunities are not always easy to predict, but they must be given attention. Factors

to be considered are availability of labor, climate, the type of commercial and industrial companies already in the area, and the rate of past business and industrial growth in the region generally.

At any particular time the economic picture may be bright or bleak depending upon the availability of money for mortgage loans and the rate of interest that must be paid to secure them. It also depends upon the availability and cost of building materials. During economic recessions, industrial and residential construction may fall to zero. In times of economic growth, new developments may appear overnight. Denominations must time the establishment of new churches accordingly.

6. Social status—"Sides of town" become socially defined so that development in a particular direction tends to have similar status to adjacent neighborhoods. The pattern may be altered, however, by topographical changes or by a large-scale developer who buys enough land to put his own imprint on the area.

7. Religious characteristics of the population—It is not possible to obtain data from the Bureau of the Census about the religious affiliation of the people in a community. Instead, information about religious preference must be secured or estimated by interviewing people in the community or checking with nearby churches. A community census may be necessary to obtain information.[4] If so, it will be time consuming, but well worth the effort. Just because a large number of people are moving into an area does not mean that a given percentage, based on other communities in the area, will be prospects for a certain denomination or congregation. It is important to know whether the new residents are drawn from other residen-

4. A community census is generally not done for a new church until it is believed that one is needed in a particular community. The census is done as part of the feasibility study (described in chapter 7) to determine whether there are enough people interested in starting a new church of that denomination. The same procedures can be used, however, in any area to gather information about the religious affiliation of a population.

tial areas of the same metropolitan area, which may be largely Roman Catholic or Jewish, or whether they are coming from other cities or rural areas.

For example, a general opinion survey across the country will probably show that most people believe that Salt Lake City has a higher percentage of Mormons than any other area. Actually, many other parts of Utah have a higher percentage of Mormons than sections of Salt Lake City. As that metropolitan area has developed, significant numbers of non-Mormons have moved in from other parts of the nation. In fact, a number of other denominations have strong churches there.

8. Ownership of property—The type of development likely to occur in a given sector, and the timing of it, often depends upon who and how many people own property there. If most of the land has been bought by a major developer or development company, construction may begin sooner than if the area is owned by a large number of people who have small amounts of acreage. A new town or planned urban development consisting of residential, commercial, and industrial tracts is possible when large tracts have been acquired.

Completing the Survey

To conclude the descriptive part of the general area survey, on one of the maps mark each elementary and junior high school in the area. These schools often show the focus or center of various residential neighborhoods.

On the same map, using a different symbol, indicate all existing churches of your denomination in the survey area and new church sites presently owned. If a black dot is used and information about the membership size of each of the churches is available, the size of the dot can be related to the size of the church. You may also want to locate on the map churches of other denominations, particularly those most like your own, and find out from each of those denominations their long-range strategies for church development. Ask about other church sites that are now owned, schedules for development, and estimates as to the membership potential of each.

Additional information about each church of your denomination will be needed. Through interviews with judicatory officials and local church representatives, you can determine the type of each church (neighborhood, metropolitan-regional, or special purpose) and the area currently served by each. It would be helpful if each church would prepare a map showing the location of the residence of each member. If this is not possible, ask the pastor and lay leaders of the individual churches to reveal those neighborhoods served in depth by each church. Then you will be able to ascertain which communities are not being served by the denomination as well as the ones in which the service areas of two or more churches overlap.

Be aware that many churches do not recognize themselves as being of one type or another. Most congregations have a few members living in all parts of the city and actually believe that they serve the whole city. Make it clear to those interviewed, therefore, if membership distribution maps cannot be obtained, that you are most interested in knowing the areas in which most of the church's members, and particularly the leaders, reside.

In addition to the location of members, obtain membership trends from each church showing the total membership size for each of the last ten to twenty years. This reveals whether the churches have been growing, declining, or maintaining the same level of membership and participation. It is helpful also to evaluate the buildings of the various churches in terms of adequacy of size, condition, and location.

Projections of Future Development

Up to this point the analysis has consisted of gathering descriptive information about the area defined for study. Some of the characteristics will remain basically unchanged for many years; others are already changing. What will the area be like in five, ten, or fifteen years? You, of course, cannot predict the future with complete accuracy, but you must try to make the best possible projections.

There are two primary concerns for exploration. First, discover the basic physical, political, economic, and land-use changes that may be anticipated. Taking the information already gathered, ask what changes are probable with regard to each part. Answers should be sought to the following questions:

How will transportation patterns be altered?

What new commercial areas will be developed?

How much new industry may be expected, and where will it be located?

What areas now designated for public use will be re-zoned for other kinds of development?

What areas will be rebuilt or renewed?

How is the political climate of the area likely to change?

What residential areas may be expected to change ra-cially or socially, and what will be their character a decade from now?

These questions are illustrative rather than comprehensive. They show the kinds of changes that may be anticipated and the types of information that will be needed.

The second major concern about the future relates to population change in the area:

Will the area have more or fewer people in a decade, and how much more or less?

How will individual neighborhoods be affected by changes in population density and mobility?

In what parts of the area will the major growth or decline take place?

How will availability of energy affect the area, particularly with regard to population change and the daily routines of the people?

If a significant number of new people are expected in the area, how will they differ from the present population in terms of religious commitment, religious affiliation, race, social class, age, marital status, and life-style?

How mobile will the citizenry be?

Will most movement take place within the area, or will many people move from the area to other areas and from other areas into this one?

How much new housing will be built and of what type?

How will zoning laws and building codes affect the future development of residential areas?

The answers to these questions may be sought from many of the same sources from which the earlier information was secured. Utility companies, especially the telephone company, may be among the most helpful, as they find it necessary to project population movements well in advance in order to anticipate needs for their services. Check also with the Chamber of Commerce, real estate agents, universities, and industrial development commissions. They may be knowledgeable, although often overly optimistic at points. Consult the city and metropolitan planning offices for anticipated changes in land use, zoning laws, and population projections. Talk to engineering firms that do studies for developers and to governmental agencies that work or operate in the area.

Publications of the United States Bureau of the Census may also provide trends regarding area growth. The managers of local industries and large commercial establishments may have access to private area development studies, which they may be willing to share. The local board of education must plan the educational needs of the area well in advance and may be able to indicate the expected location of new schools. Local and state legislative offices may provide information on pending legislation that could significantly affect the area. Ask the public library what they have in their files.

Be sure to check out all rumors about large-scale developments and special events. Many times such rumors have no basis in fact but have significant impact upon lay planning committees. Remember that any development is subject to delays and alterations. For a time in 1972–73, it was expected that the 1976 winter Olympics would be held on the western slope of the Rocky Mountains in Colorado.

Churches, schools, and various other institutions quickly developed plans in response to projected needs. Fortunately, most of that planning had not proceeded very far when the decision was made to move the Olympics elsewhere. Huge sums of money had already been spent by many groups in anticipation of the event, however. Had the political and economic overtones of the situation been better understood earlier, some mistakes and frustrations could have been avoided.

Try to discover negative factors that can block development in the area. Many of the planners and others who are interviewed will be optimistic about future developments, and perhaps only occasionally will notes of realism be injected by outsiders. Do not be misled by the idealistic optimism of others; learn to differentiate between factual information, or plans based on facts, and dreams.

Analysis of Survey Data

By the time you have reached this point in the general area survey, many weeks and even months of meeting, interviewing, exploring, and discussing will have taken place. But only the first phase of the process has been completed. While a great deal of important information will have been compiled, it is of no value unless it can be used by the church to undergird its planning and decision making. The second stage of the process, therefore, consists of analyzing and interpreting the data compiled—taking each type of information gathered and asking what it means.

Bits of information or interpretations that do not fit together, however, are not very helpful. The following general questions are offered as a framework in which the gathered information can be interpreted. As it is only a general framework, you will have to pose your own specific questions and analyze special concerns in relation to the general questions.

1. How well located are the existing congregations of

our denomination in the general survey area to serve the present and projected residential communities? In what areas are there too many churches? Where does competition exist among churches? What are the areas that we thought were covered by one of our congregations but we now find are not? What are the areas that are covered now but may not be later on as projected changes take place?

2. What is the range of ministry offered by the churches of our denomination? How many churches do we have of the various types? Do the various types of congregations complement each other or force competition with each other? What are the special opportunities of the various congregations? What are the limitations of each? (Some congregations may decide they want to remain small and become an exclusive group not open to others in their neighborhood. In another situation, a small open country church may find it impossible to minister to the residents of a new town or new suburban community developing in its area.) What other special purpose churches are needed in the area?

3. What congregations need to be closed, merged with other congregations, or relocated to other areas of the city in order to strengthen the denominational ministry to the total area?

4. Who are the people not presently served by this denomination that we can serve, should serve, and want to serve (and what are their characteristics)? (This question brings in the concern of how broadly a denomination can or should define its ministry. One denomination may find that it serves the wealthy best, yet, through guilt or genuine concern, wants to extend its ministry to lower social groups. Another denomination may find that it best attracts and serves people with lower incomes.)

5. Based on an evaluation of the relationship between existing churches and present and projected residential communities, what new congregations may be needed in the area in the next decade and where? What types of churches will be needed? What effect will each new

church have on existing congregations? What existing churches will be most able or most open to helping establish the new churches?

6. Which neighborhoods of the city, in which this denomination does not have churches, can best be served by another denomination? In what neighborhoods is our denomination strong? In which direction are residents likely to move if they begin to move toward the perimeter of the city?

7. What noncongregationally based ministries are needed in the area? Who are the people that can and should be served by our denomination but who will not voluntarily come to a church building for that service? What ministries should be the responsibility of the judicatory or a cluster of churches and, hence, may not be based in one congregation?

A Total Strategy

The need for the general area survey may be brought to the attention of the judicatory or denomination because of questions about developing new churches. However, this general area survey is intended to develop a total strategy for a denomination, not just new congregational development alone. Some judicatories include all church institutions (hospitals, homes for people with special needs, colleges, community centers, etc.) in the survey. Until the total region is looked at comprehensively, special ministries, mergers, relocations, and the development of new churches cannot be strategically planned. It may be found, for example, that the most critical areas for starting new churches during a particular period are in redeveloped areas near the core city. Or it may be found that efforts in a particular city should be directed toward supporting minority groups to develop churches. On the other hand, through mergers and relocations, areas that were thought to be in need of new churches may be better served by existing congregations.

After a total analysis and evaluation, the survey committee must decide how many new churches may be needed within a decade. In most cases the judicatory will not have sufficient funds to purchase sites for all of them, making it necessary to set priorities. Criteria used in making this judgment will include projected timing of the growth of each community, past success of this denomination in serving various types of neighborhoods, resources available, types and forms of congregations that will be needed, and how many people will be needed in a particular residential community to support the type of church anticipated. If a new metropolitan-regional church is projected for a certain part of the city, it may be that a minimum of ten thousand to twelve thousand new homes must be built over a five- to ten-year period. A special purpose church may need only a few hundred people from which to draw a congregation. A large metropolitan area may be necessary, however, for a special purpose church to draw sufficient members to be self-supporting.

Once you have analyzed the information with regard to the total denominational strategy, you, the survey committee, can present your findings with specific goals for implementation to the appropriate body. The decision-making body should act quickly to purchase needed property in recommended areas of the city. This does not mean that all of the new churches will be started, but it leaves open the option. Failure to purchase sites many years ahead of time may close the option for a particular denomination forever in certain communities.

6 : Site Selection

Based upon the findings and conclusions of the general area survey and the availability of resources, property should be purchased in those areas where a new church may be needed two to ten years hence. If it is not needed later, the property can be sold and investments made elsewhere. If a new church is needed but the character of the area changes so that the property originally bought is not well suited, it can be traded for another site, or sold and the proceeds used to purchase other property.

Judicatories that wait until it is time to organize the new church before buying a site may find that an adequate one cannot be found or is too expensive and, hence, that the development of a new congregation is not feasible. In general, an adequate site can be found if it is bought well before the area begins to develop and if the purchasers are aware of the criteria for choosing it.

The purpose of this chapter is to provide the criteria for site selection. Rarely will all of the requirements be met at an affordable price, but the person or group needs a vision of the ideals. With regard to a retail store, Edward M. Mazze says, "The recipe for an ideal store location goes something like this: Take a good piece of flat land, surround this land with many potential customers who have little access to other stores, put on this land a modern building at a low cost with all of the necessary equipment, and fill the store with excellent merchandise."[1] This recipe could be paraphrased for a church. In many cases, however, the ideal is not possible.

Paul F. Wendt points out that "It is much easier to identify the factors which should be considered in reaching a decision on location than it is to make the right decision. Every locational decision requires a forecast of the uncertain future."[2] Since church sites should be bought many years ahead of the time they will be needed, projecting the future becomes very important.

A new congregation must first determine who it wants to serve—its community. Generally, a geographical parish area extending out from the site a mile or more in each direction can be carved out as the primary drawing area for a neighborhood church. If the church wants to draw members on a basis other than geography, then that fact also will be important. The area that can be served by a church depends upon its location, transportation arteries, and travel time from residence to church location. Many churches have found that people will drive up to twenty minutes to attend church but that few will drive longer than that. People drive for longer time periods to attend a special purpose, metropolitan-regional, or downtown church than to a neighborhood church. Ten to twelve minutes may be an outside limit for travel time to a neighborhood church by new members.

Location

"It can be argued that the success of many small business firms can be expressed in one word: LOCATION."[3] "E. M. Statler once stated that the three most important

1. "Identifying the Key Factors in Retail Store Location," *Journal of Small Business Management,* January, 1972, p. 20.

2. "Deciding on Location for a Small Business," *Journal of Small Business Management,* January, 1972, p. 1.

3. *Ibid.,* p. 4.

elements for a successful hotel were 'location, location, location.' "[4] The same elements are equally valid for a church. Location is important in attracting people. Once they come voluntarily, the quality of the program becomes most important. The best program in the city, however, does not attract people if they cannot find the church.

If a church desires to be identified with a particular community (a neighborhood church), it must be located within it at a strategic spot. While people may travel outside of the local neighborhood to go to another type church (downtown, metropolitan-regional, or special purpose), they rarely go outside of their own community to a neighborhood church. The location of the church within the community determines how many people know the church exists, see it often as they go about their daily routines, or are able to get to it easily.

Visibility is one of the most important factors. The church building should be seen often by as many people as possible who live near it. The best location is on a major thoroughfare at the center or near the inner boundary of the community to be served. A corner location is much more visible than a building in the middle of a block. Sometimes, elementary schools and shopping centers have central locations in the community, and a church located near them is both centrally located and visible to people in their daily routines.

While many churches seek to save money by locating a half block or more off a main street where property values are lower, the visibility that is lost costs more than the savings on land. "Less than 100 feet often marks the difference between a good location and a bad location."[5]

Sometimes property is offered at no cost by a member or friend of the church. If such property is adequate according to the criteria discussed here, it may be wise to accept it. Often, though, it is not strategically located and is accepted only because it is free. The results are usually tra-

4. Stephen W. Brener, "Site Surveys for Successful Motels," *Journal of Small Business Management*, January, 1972, p. 37.

5. Mazze, "Identifying the Key Factors in Retail Store Location," p. 19.

gic. Cost must be only a secondary consideration in site location. A principle that should be followed is, "If a church needs a sign to direct people to it, it should be located where the sign is."

A few years ago, I flew to Omaha, Nebraska, for a consultation at a neighborhood church that was not growing. The pastor for three years of another church located within one and one-half miles of this church attempted to drive me from the airport to it. He got lost three times before he found it. He said he had been to the church before, but he got lost those times also. I knew the church's primary problem before I got there.

Another important consideration in locating a church is accessibility. How many times on a limited-access highway have you seen a motel or restaurant you wanted to patronize but were afraid that you would not be able to get back to it by the time you got to the next exit? Even though a church may be visible, if it is not also accessible, the location is not appropriate.

James Maxfield tells of visiting a church once that was located at the rear of a large lumberyard. The only access road was an unpaved driveway through the lumberyard itself. The church could not even be seen until one was well into the company's private property and had driven past many tall stacks of lumber.

The church should be approachable from at least two directions. Preferably, the site will be at the corner of a major thoroughfare and a cross street where traffic signals make it possible for people on both sides of the thoroughfare to get to the church safely. A church thus located can be seen often by new residents in the community and allows ingress and egress to the parking area from two directions.

Location in relationship to socioeconomic factors in the community is also important. A church located on the "wrong side" of a street may have difficulty reaching the target community. If the new church is intended to serve a number of smaller communities, it is best to secure a site at a neutral location. If a wide range of social classes are to be served, the church probably should be located in a neighborhood or near a neighborhood that ranks above the average. Studies have shown that people will go to a better community to go to church but not to a poorer one.

If a community is occupied by houses of many different types (including single-family homes, townhouses, apartments, condominiums, and mobile homes), it is best to locate the church in an area of single-family homes. A church located in an area of multifamily dwellings may appear to be a special purpose church and will not draw members from all parts of the community.

A church should also avoid locating in a part of the community in which nuisances may interfere with the church's ministry. Areas of extreme noise, pollution, or odors, or even areas that have a bad reputation from past use should be avoided.

While most of the characteristics listed above are equally applicable for metropolitan-regional and other types of new churches, there are some variations. A new church expected to be the metropolitan-regional type *must* be located on a main artery, usually at the intersection of two main arteries, so that it is accessible to people from a wide section of the city. Such a church may be best located at the extreme inner boundary of the area to be serviced. Few people drive away from the city to go to church. Most people go toward the downtown area. The strategically located metropolitan-regional church at the convergence of major streets at the inner boundary of the area to be served is at the "small end of the funnel" receiving people from many neighborhoods.

New churches in downtown or inner-city areas may need to be located so that many residents may walk to church. This will be particularly true of churches designed to serve compact areas of high-rise apartment buildings or condominiums.

A special purpose church designed around a particular style or issue may find that location is not as important as in other churches. Such a church is generally known by word of mouth, and people are directed to it by friends. Even this type of church, however, may find an accessible and visible location in a certain section of the city is more advantageous than a site in another neighborhood.

Size

To provide adequate space for the building, lawn, and parking, a minimum of three acres of land is recommended for a church complex. Churches in redeveloped urban areas may have to settle for less. Some can get by with two acres if they have air rights. Three acres are adequate for a church of eight hundred to one thousand members. A congregation that is expected to grow much larger than that (particularly a metropolitan-regional church) should secure five acres in the beginning except in special circumstances. Additional land may not be available later, and the church may find its growth retarded due to lack of space.

Most urban areas now require one hundred fifty to three hundred square feet of off-street parking space for every four seats in the sanctuary. Others may require one parking space for every two to five seats in the sanctuary. Enough acreage must be available.

Shape

Ideally, the shape of the church site should be a square. When that is not possible, the property may be in the shape of a rectangle as long as there is a minimum of two hundred feet of road frontage, two hundred fifty feet if possible, and there is one foot of width for every two feet of depth. Parcels of land in triangular or irregular shapes result in significant square footage being unusable and should be avoided where possible.

Topography

Property on which a church is to be located should have natural slope for drainage. It is also important that ground-level entrance ways to as many parts of the building as possible be arranged. Some churches have found it possible to have ground-level entrance ways on as many as three levels because of the slope of the property.

Proximity to flood areas and land that is lower than the street should be avoided. Property that is higher than the other property around it is to be desired. Not only are drainage and flood problems avoided, but landscape may be more beautifully accomplished. The higher the church, the more visible it is.

Soil tests should be made to assure that the property will support the buildings and that septic tanks may be used where needed. A church in a Detroit suburb once had to spend one hundred thousand dollars on cement pilings because of poor soil conditions.

Availability of Utilities

It is generally assumed that utilities (electricity, gas, water, telephone, and sewers) are or can be made available to a site. This is not always true. Many times utilities assure a potential buyer that services can be arranged only for the buyer to find at a later date that company policies have changed. Even experienced site buyers have been burned by this assumption when they bought on promises rather than hard facts or written statements.

Zoning

In some cities, churches are permitted only in certain areas. Local zoning laws should be consulted to determine whether a church can be built on the property. In some cases the church can get a variance to the zoning law when other acceptable sites cannot be found. If a variance is given, be sure to obtain it in writing rather than by the oral commitment of a municipal employee.

Ideally, the land surrounding the church for a mile or two should be primarily zoned residential. This assures that the church is located close to the residences of potential members. In no case should a church locate in or near an area that is zoned solely for industrial use or near other types of barriers or nonresidential areas. Churches located near such areas find themselves on the wrong edge rather than at the center or visible edge of the community to be served. Such locations mean that part of the parish is cut off from easy access to the church. In addition, industrial properties frequently have a negative influence on the residential neighborhood.

Cost

Corner property on main thoroughfares costs plenty. It is not unusual today for churches to pay fifty thousand to one hundred thousand dollars or more for such sites. As pointed out earlier, however, the more expensive property may be the best buy in terms of its impact on the growth of the church.

There are times when ideal sites are available but only at prohibitive costs. In no case should churches pay more than property is worth or give in to scalpers. Judicatories are often well advised to engage a professional appraiser in cases where large sums are involved and the value of property is difficult to determine. An Episcopal diocese on the East Coast recently was offered a seven-acre tract of land for a new church for three hundred fifty thousand dollars. The investigation of an appraiser found, however, that the land was significantly overpriced and recommended that two hundred twenty-five thousand dollars be offered for it.

Title

When a site is purchased, the church or judicatory should receive a fee simple title, which means that ownership of the property is free and clear of all encumbrances. A title search should be made to determine the existence of any flaws, easements, right-of-ways, or covenants that "run with the land." If such restrictions may have an adverse effect on the use of the land for a church site, do not buy the land. Have an attorney examine the title report. If future widening of or relocation of public roads is likely to encroach on the site, this also should be taken into consideration. Such changes may enhance the value and utility of the site, but they may also have the opposite effect.

Land titles with reversionary clauses in the deed should not be accepted. In many cases congregations have accepted gifts of land with title restrictions that provide for its return to the donor (or his or her heirs) if the property ceases to be used by the church. Such a restriction means that the church does not have a merchantable title, and it will not be able to secure a first mortgage loan.

Availability of Public Transportation

As shortage of energy may cause a decrease in the use of automobiles, and as new churches are developed in areas other than suburbs, availability of public transportation and mass transit will be increasingly important. Sites that are well located with regard to transit routes will have an advantage.

Currently, few people go to church by public transportation due both to the infrequency of Sunday morning transit schedules as well as the convenience of automobiles. New York City is probably the only city where a significant number of people use mass transit to get to church, simply because of scarcity and cost of parking. As other cities become as dense as major metropolitan areas such as New York, the automobile will become a liability in them also.

Distance to Other Churches

In general a new church should not be located closer than four miles to another church of the same denomination. Of course, the type of churches and breadth of communities served will be the primary determining factors.

With regard to proximity to churches of other denominations, one denominational church planner has recommended that a minimum of one mile distance separate the churches. We doubt that such an admonition is necessary or acceptable. If there is need for both churches in the community, it is as acceptable for them to be located next door or across the street from one another as to be several blocks or miles apart. If one church has a good, central, visible and accessible location, a church of another denomination located near it will also have these qualities. If competition exists between the congregations, it will not be caused by their being located near each other or eliminated by their being far apart.

An Important Decision

Once a piece of property has been bought and the church constructs its first building unit, it has little choice but to stay at that site for a generation or more. Therefore, the importance of selecting the right site cannot be overestimated. The church that locates well reaps the benefits throughout its lifetime. The church that locates poorly lives to regret it, or dies because of it.

7 : The Feasibility Study

The general area survey has been completed. If this was accomplished many years before and has been updated every two or three years, target areas for new churches will have been chosen and, we would hope, sites will have been purchased. If the general area survey has only recently been completed, sites for new churches in designated areas may now be in the process of negotiation. In either case, it may be that a particular segment of the survey area is developing with new homes, and the time may be right for the organization of a new church. It may be a community that was not noticed before in the general area survey or one that was given low priority because it was not expected to develop quickly. In this case a site may not now be owned, and the search for one may have to go on simultaneously with other activities.

It is now time for a feasibility study to see if conditions call for the establishment of a new church and, if so, the proper timing for its organization. The discussion in this chapter is intended to guide the person or group responsible for new church development in making the decision. This decision will be one of the most crucial in the entire church development process.

Let us be clear about the difference between the general area survey and the feasibility study. The purpose of the former is much broader than the latter. The general area survey covers a large geographical area including many neighborhoods. It is done for the purpose of working out a general denominational strategy for ministering to the area. It is a broad survey using specific data to establish general guidelines for future decisions. The feasibility study, on the other hand, is limited, in most cases, to one particular community or segment of the larger area originally surveyed. It is for the specific purpose of determining whether a new church is needed and, if so, the right time for launching it. The feasibility study will also take into consideration the larger ministry of the denomination in the area but only with regard to how it affects and is affected by decisions regarding a new church in a specific community.

Possible Conclusions

Before discussing the specifics of how to conduct a feasibility study, let's consider the four types of conclusions that may be reached:

1. A new church of this denomination will not be needed in this community. The neighborhood may have developed, or failed to develop, in such a way that a church should not be organized. If a site had been purchased previously, it may now be sold and the attention of the denomination turned elsewhere.

2. It is still too early to make a decision. In this case the "jury is still out." There may be further growth in the community which, if it continues, may call for the establishment of a new church later, but it should not be started now. If a site is owned, it should be reappraised in the light of changes that have taken place, and possibly traded for another one. In any case it will not be used now or sold. The area will continue to be watched.

3. A new church will be needed, but now is not the proper time. This is a positive response to the criteria used in the feasibility study with the exception of the timing. It

is concluded that this denomination should have a ministry here, but it is too early to tell what kind or to gather more specific data about the community. Again, the denomination should reappraise the site for the new church and act immediately to secure another site if the original one is found to be poorly located. The priority assigned to this community for new church development in the beginning may need to be adjusted.

4. A new church is needed, and now is the time to proceed. In this case the judicatory or denomination must begin immediately to prepare a mission design, search for an organizing pastor, and secure financing.

Need for a New Congregation

We can now return to the beginning to understand how one or another of these conclusions may be reached. The first question to be answered is whether a new church is needed. If the answer is yes, the question of timing can then be considered.

The decision about whether to proceed should be based on a reappraisal of the factors considered in the general area survey, but primarily with regard to those which affect the particular community. The feasibility study committee will be looking for significant changes in land use, population projections, the political and economic climate, and so on. Specific questions to be asked include the following:

1. How many people live in the community now? What is the ultimate population of the community now expected to be, and how rapidly will it grow?

2. How mobile is this community?

3. Who are the people moving in? Are they primarily young families, middle-aged couples, the elderly, or singles? What life-styles may be discerned? What is the racial character of the community? What is the income and education level of the adults?

4. What types of housing are being constructed and in

what proportion? Will the community be diverse or basically homogeneous?

5. Have elementary schools already been constructed and where are they located?

6. What shopping areas have been provided for the new community? Have they already been built or how soon may they be expected? Where will people go to shop if such facilities will not be available locally?

7. Where do the people who live in this area work? If it is primarily outside of the community, to what other areas do they go?

8. Are all utilities now available or can they reasonably be expected to be added as needed?

9. Has an additional primary barrier, such as a major thoroughfare or limited access highway, been created, which divides the community?

10. What is the present availability of mortgage money and building materials? Is a period approaching when residential construction is likely to be halted for a time?

11. What is the reputation of this community in the rest of the city? Is it seen as a desirable or undesirable place to live? Does its development have the support of political leaders? How have zoning and building laws been altered in a way that benefits this neighborhood?

12. Is there reason to believe that the religious character of the new residents is different than in the area generally?

13. What other mainline churches have already organized?

14. How close are other viable churches of the denomination to the proposed site of the new church? How will they be affected by the new church based on present evidence? Are any of them now attracting new members from this community in significant numbers?

The answers to these questions and others that may be asked will determine whether a new church is needed in a specific community now. Some information, such as the rate of population growth and type of housing, may be more important than other data. The answers will have to be compared and finally evaluated as objectively as possible. No mathematical formula can be given for making the decision. In few communities will all of the criteria be positive. We have never seen a group, however, that was aware of the criteria for making the right decision fail to do so.

Timing

If the decision that results from the feasibility study is to proceed, the question of timing becomes crucial. The following basic rules of thumb may be helpful:

1. The community at the time the decision is made to proceed should have a minimum population of fifteen hundred people in the case of a neighborhood church that is expected to reach self-support within five to seven years. It should reasonably expect to have a minimum of eighty to one hundred members within one year from the date of the first worship service. Most metropolitan-regional churches should have one hundred fifty or more by that time. Many special purpose churches, on the other hand, may find that fifty members during the first year is a worthy goal. If these minimum membership levels cannot be attained, it may be too early to start gathering the congregation. Regardless of the type of church, people want to be part of a congregation that has potential and shows signs of being permanent. Image is an important factor. A congregation that portrays an image of being a growing and alert institution makes a positive impression in the community.

2. The growth of the community should be continuing. Realistic population projections should show that a neighborhood church can expect three hundred to five hundred members in seven to ten years. A metropolitan church should be expected to have twice or three times that number at the end of ten to twelve years. Most special purpose churches should have potential of growth to at least two hundred if self-support is expected. Generally, a denomina-

tion can estimate the percentage of population in an area that is now of a particular denomination and expect that increases will continue in the same proportion. Caution is in order, however, for areas that may be developing with a strong concentration of people who are not of that denomination.

3. The majority of the residents in the community should have lived in their present homes for less than three years. Most people living in an area for longer than that have established themselves in another congregation or have become confirmed nonchurchgoers. Once the people have related themselves to another congregation, formed friendships, and taken on responsibilities, it is difficult to attract them to the new congregation. Sometimes a nearby church of the same denomination will encourage members living in the area of the new church to transfer. If such can be expected, the importance of this factor may be reduced. However, if a majority of the people living in the area have been there three or more years and other churches of the denomination are not encouraging members in the area to transfer to the new church, the population of the new community at the time the new congregation is launched should be much more than fifteen hundred.

The number of residents in a community is easily discernible. The number of occupied single-family housing units may be counted and multiplied by the average number of persons per family—generally 2.97. Multiply multi-family housing units by 2.3.

The number of new residents who are already members of other churches or are open to participation in a new church within the community may not be so easily known. For this information the denomination or sponsoring agency for the new church will have to conduct a door-to-door community survey. Generally, this is the last step in determining the feasibility of starting a new congregation and the proper timing for it. For some denominations, however, it is the first step undertaken by the mission developer (pastor) when he or she arrives on the scene. In this case, generally a decision to send in a developer is different than a decision to organize a congregation. The latter decision is made after the developer has made in-depth interviews and a thorough study of the community.

Community Survey

The purpose of the community survey is to gather information about the denominational profile of the community, the number of families already related to other local churches, the number of persons or families interested in participating in starting a new congregation of this denomination, and general information about these persons or families.

The community survey may be conducted in either of two ways. Every family may be contacted so that every home in the community is covered. An alternative to a complete survey is a random sample survey according to a carefully predetermined plan, such as knocking on every fourth or fifth door in the community. In the latter case it will be assumed that the information gathered from the sampled families may be extended to include those not questioned; that is, the data can be multiplied by four or five. If resources and canvassers are available, it is strongly suggested that the complete door-to-door community survey be used, even if the area to be covered has to be reduced. It provides more complete and accurate data, and the names can be used later by the pastor in gathering the congregation.

Much of the adequacy and reliability of the information from the survey will be determined by the preparation that is done ahead of time. Many details must be taken care of before the date that the survey takes place.

Workers, to carry out the survey, can usually be recruited from nearby churches. These churches should be kept informed and urged to participate in all preliminary planning for the new congregation. There is no reason that the feasibility study cannot be accomplished at one time for all of the denominations considering starting a new church in the area. As a matter of fact, it is one of the best occasions for churches of all denominations to participate in extending the church to a nearby new community.

To determine the number of workers necessary to cover the new community (which will be clearly defined ahead of time), divide the total number of dwelling units by twenty-five. One person can generally cover that many homes in one and a half hours of canvass time. An additional half hour to forty-five minutes of orientation time should be planned for workers before the actual survey begins. In many communities Sunday afternoon is a good time.

Workers may go out in teams, with each team assigned fifty homes to be surveyed in a clearly defined part of the survey area. Each person should wear a name tag as identification. One team member can work one side of the street while the other person works the other side. In many surveys canvassers have been provided folders with information about plans for the new church, which can be left in each home where interest is expressed. Survey cards with the questions to be asked and information to be gathered must be printed ahead of time. The survey card should include all questions to be asked and space for responses. In addition to name, address, and denominational membership or preference, the most important question to be asked is, Would you be interested in participating in the development of a new church in this community? If the answer is affirmative, the canvasser should ask which denomination would be preferred. Space should also be allowed on the survey card for the canvasser's own evaluation of the interest shown or special situations revealed by residents.

As survey cards are returned to the central location, results can be tabulated in terms of the total number of people interested in a new congregation, number of persons with preference for each denomination, number of families not at home, and number of vacant homes. Families that were not at home on the first try should be visited again at least once within the following week. In analyzing the results of the survey, remember that only about 50 percent of the people who answer "yes" or "undecided" to the question of whether they would be interested in participating in the development of a new congregation of a certain denomination will actually become members of the new church in the first year. Further, one cannot assume that all or even most people now holding membership in or preference for a particular denomination will become involved in the new church.

Except in special purpose churches, past studies have shown that two-thirds to three-fourths of the first year's membership in a new church have had previous membership in that denomination. Generally, 20 percent are from other denominations, and 10 percent have not had any prior religious affiliation. In later years of a church's life, a larger percentage of new members can be expected to be new converts.

The Decision to Proceed

Following the update of the general area survey and the testing of specific criteria in the community under consideration, the survey usually provides the additional data needed to decide if a new church should be organized and when. There is no way to be absolutely sure that the decision to launch a new congregation is a wise one. But when the decision is made using the most reliable data available, there is a good basis for the decision and few wrong ones are made.

8 : The Preliminary Mission Design

What Is It?

When the feasibility study has been completed and a decision has been made to proceed with the organization of a new church, the next step is the preparation of a design for the new congregation and its ministry. If the community is now ready for a new church, delay of only a few months may be harmful. Work should begin as soon as possible to secure an organizing pastor, make arrangements for a temporary meeting place, and purchase or repurchase a site if an adequate one has not already been bought and it is believed that one is needed. These steps cannot be carried out adequately, however, until the person or group responsible for the organization of the new congregation has made firm decisions about the type of new congregation needed, its goals, funding, and how it will carry out its task. These are the primary ingredients of the preliminary mission design.

The person or group doing the advance preparation for a new congregation has a responsibility to define clearly in a written document (the preliminary mission design) the type of congregation to be organized and its initial goals. This document should state what is expected of the new congregation during the first year and detail what can logically be expected from the judicatory and denomination during this period.

96

The preliminary mission design is the first step in helping a new congregation to develop such an identity for itself. The pastor and the residents of the community will then have an understanding of what this particular new church will be like and what to expect of it.

A preliminary design fills three basic needs. It is: (1) a guide for obtaining approval from appropriate persons or judicatory and denominational boards and committees; (2) a "job description" that may be used in the search for an organizing pastor; and (3) a definition of goals toward mission that the organizing pastor can use in issuing invitations to people to be a part of the new congregation.

A carefully prepared preliminary design document helps to avoid misunderstandings between the pastor, congregation, and judicatory. It also serves as a basis for evaluating the progress of the congregation at the end of the first six months and the first year.

The original mission design should not be considered final for the life of the congregation. A two-stage process is suggested. The first stage (the preliminary mission design and the one under discussion here) should be completed by a carefully selected group of people well before the church is organized. It consists of denominational goals for the new church, not those of the people who will ultimately participate in it. The second stage (the congregation's mission design, which is discussed in chapter 11) is drafted when the new congregation has begun to gather and worship and is preparing to become an organized or chartered congregation. The final mission design may be negotiated with the judicatory, but it is primarily the responsibility of the indigenous congregation. Actually the mission statement should be revised periodically and updated throughout the life of the congregation.

The preliminary mission design should be prepared by a carefully selected team of persons: (1) the persons, or representatives from the groups, who conducted the most recent update of the general area survey and the feasibility study of the community; (2) at least two residents from the new community known to be interested in participating in the new congregation; (3) the pastors of the two nearest congregations of the church's denomination; (4) the judicatory executive or denominational representative; (5) a representative from the judicatory or denominational agency or committee responsible for new church development in the area (if any); and (6) a representative of the finance board or committee that will have responsibility for allocating funds for the new congregation.

Additional people may be added from the community or the judicatory because of their responsibilities, interest, or special expertise.

The preliminary mission design should not be a lengthy document that few people will read. It can be kept to a maximum of five pages using brief and succinct statements to summarize the intentions for the new congregation.

Content of the Design

Because the actual contents of the mission design vary from place to place, a standardized form is inappropriate. As it is essential that the character of this new congregation be tailored for the particular area that it serves, it may even be recommended that the mission design committee not have similar documents from other congregations before them as they work. The following are suggested contents to be included in most well-intentioned and carefully thought-out design statements:

1. A brief recount of the factors uncovered in the general area survey and feasibility study, which led to the decision to organize a new congregation. This statement shows why the congregation is needed at this time.

2. A brief theological statement undergirding the concepts that prompted the decision to launch the new congregation. The committee needs to show that the decision to proceed was not based only on the fact that a strong social institution could be established that would attract a large

number of members. It should show that the religious needs of the community to be served have been carefully considered.

3. The purpose of the new congregation within the context of a denominational strategy for the larger area in which it is located. It must be shown that other churches will not have the capacity to serve this area in the way a new congregation will, that it is better to start a new congregation than to relocate an existing one, and that the funds expended have been considered in conjunction with all mission needs in the area.

4. The type of congregation to be organized. The committee preparing the mission design is the proper group to designate whether this local church should be a neighborhood church, a metropolitan-regional church, a downtown church, a special purpose church, and so on. The feasibility study will have shown the need for one or another of these types. If the church is to be a special purpose church, the specific purpose, style, or issue that the congregation will be gathered around should be defined. This statement should also indicate whether the new congregation will have a building, be experimental, appeal to a particular core age-group, be ecumenical, or be intended for a particular racial or ethnic group.

5. Suggestion of areas in which the congregation is expected to concentrate its life and witness, such as worship, social ministry, Christian nurture, mission activities, and so on.

6. Suggested goals that will help the new congregation to build a strong social institution during the first year. These goals should be specific, attainable, and measurable and should be stated with regard to membership, finances, program, community involvement, and organizational structure.

7. Suggested programs and strategies for attaining these goals. Included will be pastoral and lay visitation, stewardship, education, lay training, and so on.

8. Specific social problems that the new congregation will be able to help resolve. A new church in a transitional community, for example, may be especially concerned with racial issues or adequate housing. A new suburban congregation may have special responsibility in the areas of family relations, marriage counseling, alcoholism, or open housing.

9. The role of the pastor in the new congregation. It should be recognized that the role of the pastor in a new church is different from his role in an established one.

10. Relationships with churches of other denominations that will be serving the same community.

11. Delineation of clear lines of responsibility and communication between the congregation and the judicatory or denomination.

12. Assistance that the new congregation can expect from the judicatory and existing neighboring churches.

13. Sources of financial support and the length of time that the congregation can expect subsidy.

14. Arrangements for a temporary meeting place or alternatives to be considered by the congregation itself. As with most other factors, the final decision will be reserved to the congregation.

15. Finally, it is important that all arrangements, deals, understandings, and contracts made by the judicatory or denomination before the congregation is organized be clearly delineated in the mission design. This will help to avoid embarassing the judicatory or the congregation at a later time.

The preliminary mission design is a blueprint of what the organizing body expects in the new institution. Without it, the new congregation may flounder and suffer throughout its lifetime for lack of a clearly defined purpose and identity.

In no way is the preliminary mission design intended to set immovable parameters in which the new congregation must operate. It is a guide to assist the congregation as it begins to think about its life as the people of God in a specific place.

9 : Financing the New Congregation

Mission, as the term is used in the Christian Church, is sharing. By it existing religious fellowships share their faith through providing for the religious needs of people in other communities. The existing fellowships help others start churches that meet their needs so that they also can share. Where inadequate initial support results in weak congregations, the future extension of the church and sharing of the gospel is sacrificed. No denomination should establish more new congregations than it can adequately support during the congregations' infancy. It is better to establish fewer strong congregations than to create more than can be supported and risk failure in all of them.

The Cost of a New Church

From numerous studies of new church funding policies over the last two decades and their consequences, we can get a realistic picture of the initial cost of a new congregation, the important role of the judicatory or denomination in supporting the new church, and the financial responsibility that should be carried by the new congregation itself.

It is difficult to estimate the total cost of establishing a new church. Land values, salaries, supplies, and services vary widely according to region, location within a metropolitan area, the character of the community, and the kind

101

of congregation to be organized. Many experienced new church developers warn that a denomination should not organize a new congregation unless it is prepared to subsidize the congregation a minimum of ninety thousand to one hundred fifty thousand dollars during its first five years. (The exceptions to this are some special purpose churches that are expected to have unusually low overhead, and ecumenical congregations in which a number of denominations share the costs.) Some new congregations require a subsidy of two hundred thousand dollars or more from the denomination plus the amount that is raised by the congregation itself during this period. One Midwestern judicatory recently paid one hundred sixty thousand dollars for a four-acre site. Another within 125 miles of it purchased an equally choice five-acre site for seventy thousand dollars.

New downtown and metropolitan-regional churches are generally the most expensive because of the need for prime locations, which also are desirable to commercial establishments. Neighborhood churches often have to pay forty thousand to fifty thousand dollars or more for a good site. With the use of multipurpose facilities, the initial subsidy for such churches can sometimes be held to one hundred thousand dollars. Most new churches in small towns and open country areas have similar costs. Since special purpose churches have such a broad range, it is difficult to estimate their costs. House churches and small congregations gathered around specific issues or styles may find it possible to forego the purchase of a site and construction of a building, but subsidy may be needed for pastoral salary.

Time Period for Subsidy

Five years is the average time span for outside financial assistance. The actual time is best determined by periodic evaluations participated in by representatives of the judicatory and the congregation. Such evaluations should be held at least annually and probably twice each year during the first two years. The primary concern is to make sure that the congregation is carrying its fair share financially without being under an excessive financial burden. A new United Methodist church in the South held its first worship service in October, 1974, was chartered in March, 1975, and became self-supporting with 171 members by June of that year. Few churches can do that well, and most should not be expected to do so.

Generally it is expected that financial assistance will be given on a descending scale. Most of the expenses should be paid by outside funds during the first six months. During each successive year, the congregation should accept proportionately more responsibility.

In many cases the amount of duration of subsidy will be determined by the social level of the community served by a new congregation. For example, Philip Park, a church development officer in the United Presbyterian Church, tells of organizing a new Korean congregation a few years ago that had eighty medical doctors in the membership. He concluded that subsidy may not have been needed in that congregation at all.[1]

On the other hand, it should not be assumed that new churches organized in poor or lower-class communities should receive mission congregation status or large initial subsidies. Mr. Park goes on:

As far as money issues are concerned, no project should be funded on a long term basis. I once served a congregation in Pittsburgh which was begun on the basis of strong financial support from the judicatory and has continued on that basis. Part of the difficulty here is that the church is primarily made up of persons who live in low income public housing, so that support of a particular style of ministry which is common in my denomination was not easy for them. That church has been on

1. Philip Kyung Sik Park, "Factors in Racial Church Development."

support for 16 years, and unless strategies change, it may always be supported. That is a most unfortunate situation for several reasons. One, it ignores church styles which do not exist in the judicatory but which do exist in the racial community which that church represents. Secondly, that judicatory has never reflected on what being on the "dole" has meant for that congregation and for a people who also may be on some form of public assistance. It might be important for them to realize that they can support a church, albeit at a somewhat different style, even when they are incapable of supporting themselves.[2]

Financing new congregations is a delicate matter. Some are allowed to starve until they can support themselves, if they ever do. Others are given such large subsidies (although it does not happen too often) that they develop a dependency psychology, which may be difficult to overcome in later years. This dependency syndrome may cause a congregation to remain small and prohibit it from ever becoming self-supporting. However, the congregation should not be pushed so hard that it becomes incapacitated and overly concerned with finances during its first critical years.

Responsibility of the Denomination

The funding policies of denominations vary significantly. Some provide more subsidy for certain items and less for others. For example, some pay the entire cost of the site; some consider it a part of a capital loan along with buildings; and others make a grant to the church for a portion of the cost.

In determining the amount of subsidy needed for a particular new congregation, the denomination or judicatory generally should assume responsibility for the following items or their equivalent:

1. The site. In those cases where the site was purchased several years before the congregation is established, its

2. *Ibid.*

cost may not be considered a part of the subsidy required to organize the new congregation. When it must be purchased at the time the new congregation is started, it is one of the largest cost factors, and usually the total cost should be the responsibility of the judicatory.

2. The organizing pastor's salary and fringe benefits (including utilities, travel allowance, insurance, and housing allowance if a church-owned home is not bought). The judicatory should have full responsibility for these costs for the first year and partial responsibility on a descending scale for the next four years.

3. Home for the pastor. If a parsonage (rectory, manse) is to be purchased, the denominational subsidy should provide for the down payment, mortgage and insurance payments on the house, and furnishings for the first year. If it will not be furnished, an adequate allowance to cover the down payment of needed appliances should be provided.

4. Facilities for worship and church school during the first six months. This includes rental of a community facility or space in another church, or the full cost of other temporary facilities, particularly if they will later be used by the judicatory in another place. If the first unit of the permanent building is erected before the congregation is organized, or during the first year, then the down payment, mortgage payments, and insurance for the first year should be provided by the denomination.

5. Costs related to the feasibility study and community survey. Included in this expense are the cost of printing brochures and survey cards, purchase of maps and incidentals.

6. Minimum office equipment and supplies (including mimeograph machine, typewriter, postage, mailing permit, telephone, bulletin covers, letterheads, etc.), secretarial assistance, and an office/study apart from the pastor's residence for the first year. This expense may be reduced when nearby churches invite the new church to use their office equipment, office staff, or provide office space during the early months.

Responsibility of the Congregation

From the time it is officially organized, and to some degree from the time of the first worship service, the congregation should begin contributing to operating costs. All expenses not listed above should be the local church's responsibility. In addition to local expenses, the new church should begin to contribute to the basic benevolence program of the denomination by the end of the first quarter. The amount contributed should increase in each succeeding quarter until an annual budget is established.

Generally the budget for the first six months of the church's life is prepared by the judicatory executive or group responsible for the establishment of the new church. The sources of income should be listed with the specific amount from each, including the portion that the new congregation will raise itself. The budget for the second six-month period should be prepared jointly by the judicatory and the new congregation.

Until the new church has been duly constituted, the treasurer of the judicatory or a designated representative often receives and disperses funds. As soon as a treasurer is elected by the new church at the time of organization, all funds should be channeled through that person. This enables the new congregation to see at an early stage how much money it takes to operate a church. At the same time, it gives the church's official governing body the responsibility for managing the money. It enables the members to be aware of the sources of outside income and the fact that other churches are giving them substantial help. The church treasurer should prepare a complete financial statement each quarter and distribute it to all contributors.

The financial responsibility of the congregation begins at the time of organization and increases until self-support is attained at the end of five years or the designated time. If the church grows as expected and adequate planning has been done, the church should not find it difficult to accept these financial commitments as they come due.

Throughout the first decade of the church's life many costs are related to development. Consequently, the church is tempted at times to delay increasing its giving to benevolences until other costs are reduced. Where this thinking predominates, the church usually lags behind in its mission involvement. Failure to increase its participation in the larger ministry of the church each year may be a sign that the church has forgotten its formal purpose and goals and is overly concerned with survival.

The new church should begin its stewardship program at the time the church is constituted. Each member, beginning with the charter members, should be given an opportunity to make a pledge so that the church may plan its budget. As they join, new members should be given the same opportunity. Additional stewardship programs should be held annually.

At the end of the first year, when two budget periods of six months duration each have ended, the congregation should be able to make up an annual budget on its own. Continuing subsidy from the denomination can be considered as one source of income along with the members' contributions.

Provision should be made for the pastor's salary to be reviewed annually. Some pastors are reluctant to accept an appointment or call to a new church because they believe the salary will be locked in by the denomination. In many cases the judicatory reduces the support for salary by the amount of the increase accepted by the congregation. In this instance the pastor does not receive a raise until the total responsibility for salary is taken by the church. If the congregation and the judicatory believe that the pastor deserves a raise (whether merit or cost-of-living) each year, provision should be made for it at the time the financial plan for the new church is adopted.

10 : Selection of the First Pastor

Many stages make up the long and complex process of developing a new church. Some follow logically after other stages have been completed, but at many points a number of interrelated processes are going on simultaneously. The quality of the work done in one stage and the decisions made in relation to it have long-range repercussions for other parts and for the quality and success of the whole endeavor.

Two Key Roles

There are two roles, filled by two different persons, through which the total process is managed. The abilities of these persons are keys to the success of the project.

The first key role is filled by the denominational representative, judicatory executive, chairperson of the church extension committee, or representative from the nearby mother church who has primary responsibility for the process discussed up to this point. This person will have led, participated in, or reviewed the general area survey; bought or appraised the site for the new church; directed the feasibility study; taken primary responsibility for the preparation of the mission design; and arranged financing for the new church. If the process has broken down or been circumvented to this point, it may be irreparably harmed. If these tasks have been done well, the project will have a good foundation. This person will now be responsible for writing a job description and selecting the first pastor for the new church.

The selection of the first pastor, the second key role, will be the final major responsibility of the judicatory representative. This does not mean that he or she will no longer be involved. With the selection of the pastor, however, the pastor becomes the leader in the continuing development of the new congregation. Thus, this final major task of the judicatory executive is doubly crucial. Whether the pastor will be appointed or called by the judicatory, the appropriate person must be found. Even more than other crucial decisions that have been made, such as the decision to proceed and site selection, *selection of the right pastor is the single most important factor.*

The responsibilities and duties of the pastor are so diverse that one or a few criteria will not be sufficient. He or she will be more than just the manager of the organization. As organizer, developer, and catalyst, he will actually call the new institution into being. The imprint of his personality and skills more than that of any other one person will be indelibly inscribed in the fabric of the new congregation. Even more than in established congregations, he will be the center, focus, and primary tangible symbol of the gathering congregation in its early days.

The pastor must be selected solely on the basis of his suitability for this particular new church. It cannot be a political appointment in which someone's best friend or "favorite son" is selected because he deserves a promotion, has a pleasing personality, or fills a quota. He must not be chosen because he is out of a job or would like to move from another position. At a time when there is an oversupply of white and Asian clergy, there is often a temptation to select a person to lead the new church who is unemployed or is just entering the ministry. In most cases these are negative rather than positive characteristics.

Among some minorities, the problem is the opposite. There is a serious shortage of trained clergy among blacks, Hispanics, and Native Americans in this country in mainline Protestant denominations, particularly the predominantly white denominations. Finding qualified people in these groups to serve as organizing pastors of new churches may appear at times to be impossible.

Qualities of Effective New Church Pastors

What are the qualities and skills desirable for the pastor of a new congregation? This question does not have an easy answer. Each person who has had experience with new congregations could put together a list that would differ from the others. Many traits desirable for a new church pastor would also be appropriate for the pastor of any church. In making an evaluation sheet, there is a temptation to list every characteristic generally held to be desirable in any pastor, and to urge the person or group responsible for making the selection to find the "perfect" pastor.

This has not been the course chosen here. Based upon the experience of studying scores of new churches over the past five years, the following list has been compiled. These qualities are uniquely important for a new church pastor or are judged to be more important for the pastor of a new church than for clergy generally.

First, we shall refer to those attributes that may have wide applicability to most pastors but whose importance cannot be overlooked in the selection of the pastor for a new congregation. They are as follows:

1. Personal religious commitment. The new church pastor must be committed to the faith to which he seeks to lead others. He must have an "evangelistic" concern that persons now outside the church have the opportunity of participating in the Christian life through the acceptance of Jesus Christ as Lord and Savior. He must have a faith that demands to be shared.

2. An understanding of the primary task of a pastor. In a

new church the pastor needs to be realistic about his job as developer and manager of a social institution, but he must also recognize and understand the priestly role that the pastor alone carries. This includes accepting people where they are, with the burdens they carry, and helping them through worship and nurture to find meaning for their lives, thus enabling them to operate as "whole persons" in society. While change and growth in people's lives is to be sought, the pastor must understand that real and meaningful change comes only as a result of a person's recognition of acceptance by God and the Christian community. G. Lloyd Rediger expressed this concept helpfully in a discussion of the change agent model of ministry: "Most of us would agree that much needs to be changed in the church and community. The difficulty lies in the tyranny of the thought process for the pastor who takes on the change agent role. He/she may begin to preach, teach, counsel and serve in a forcing, manipulative manner. He/she is increasingly unable to meet people where they are. For where they are needs to be changed. He/she expects them to move to his/her viewpoint and behavior. The people he/she serves may actually become the enemy in his/her thinking."[1]

3. Capacity to utilize resources. In the early days of a new congregation there will be few material or human resources. The pastor of an infant organization must be persuasive and adept in evoking the best in people and enabling the early members to do many tasks for which they may not have had prior training or experience. The pastor must be capable of forming groups and working in and through them to accomplish their stated purpose and goals.

4. Good interpersonal relating style. In addition to understanding the needs of people, the pastor must have the ability to show appreciation and support for persons as

1. "The Change Agent Model: Some Practical Considerations," *Christian Ministry*, January, 1974, p. 32.

persons. He must be open, accessible, and sensitive to the needs of members and residents of the community.

5. Creativity. A new congregation does not have a tradition upon which its future can be built. The pastor must be capable of envisioning the end-product of the organization that is being created. He will be capable of putting together a blueprint for the church that can be shared with the members and can be tested and modified by the total group until a common vision and common goals are brought forth.

6. Basic skills in leading worship, preaching, planning and goal setting, and stewardship and finance.

In addition to those qualities a new church pastor should have *in common* with his colleagues, there are *unique* attributes that the pastor in a new congregation should possess:

1. Training and experience. The new church pastor should have a seminary education and other training (courses in management, interpersonal relationships, etc.) and experience that have prepared him for this unique task. Few can do a good job as pastor of a new church if this is the first pastoral experience. It is difficult to learn how to be a pastor at the same time the congregation is learning how to be a church. It is better if the person chosen has had at least two good experiences previously as pastor of established churches. Such a person will understand the dynamics of a congregation and will have more than one model of a congregation from which to draw. There are few retired persons who will have enough energy and flexibility to handle the task and few recent seminary graduates with sufficient experience.

2. Trainable. Due to the unique nature of a new church, few pastors will have all of the training and skills needed to carry out the task. Although the person chosen will be highly skilled and experienced, he will recognize personal limitations. He will know what he does not know and will periodically seek training in those areas.

3. Recognition of interdependence. Once selected, the

new pastor must recognize that primary responsibility for the success of the new congregation, on the human level, is in his hands. He will understand the cooperative nature of the venture, however, and be willing to work with and to a large extent under the guidance of judicatory or denominational supervisors. The pastor will be open to suggestions from the higher officials and open his work to review and evaluation.

Preliminary work done by the judicatory, or other body, in the general area survey, feasibility study, and mission design should be shared with pastoral candidates before the selection is made. His ability to accept these findings, to recognize the uniqueness of the community, to relate to the preliminary mission design, to test it against his own understanding of the community to be served, and to recognize the type and form of church needed in the area will be important criteria of the person's acceptability for the task. A pastor who feels the previous spadework should be ignored or is in error should be bypassed. The desirable person is one who accepts the preliminary work but is not limited by it and is willing to test the appropriateness of the design as he begins to work in the community.

4. Appreciation of the church as an institution and optimism about its future. It is impossible to be at basic odds with the established church and develop a new congregation that will be a part of it. People who believe that the church is dying, has already died, has lost its purpose, is powerless, or is irrelevant to contemporary society will be neither happy, fulfilled, nor productive in this capacity. On the other hand, a pastor should not be sought who blindly accepts the established church as being coterminus with the Kingdom of God in the world. The new church pastor should be one who recognizes the church's faults but who is confident about the possibility of its renewal in every age.

5. Aggressiveness, issuing in the ability to face problems directly, and accomplish stated goals. The new church pastor has no congregation. The pastor must be

willing himself to aggressively recruit the congregation through a priority on calling and pastoral visitation during the early years. A pastor whose concept is "being the church" rather than "building the church" would be more appropriately deployed elsewhere.

6. Personal stability. At a time when there are few signs of stability and permanence in the congregation, the pastor will himself need to be an essentially stable person. For the first few critical months, about the only stable aspect of a new church is the pastor.

7. A self-starter. He cannot be dependent emotionally upon someone else. The emotional needs of the new congregation weigh most heavily upon him. Unless he has the ability to deal with his own emotions, to make decisions and follow through, he will not be able to carry the added burden.

8. Supportive family. During the first year or so the new church pastor will spend long hours in organizing the new church. Pastoral calling and meetings occupy many evenings in addition to the daylight hours. If the pastor is to do a good job in this task, his family (if there is one) must recognize the unique responsibility he carries for this period. The pastor should, however, recognize the necessity and importance of having at least one day each week apart from the demanding duties of organizing the congregation.

The perfect pastor, one who has all or even most of the qualities listed above, does not exist. As Frank C. Williams, in a study for the American Lutheran Church, points out, "Because human beings are so wonderfully complex, no system or process of hiring personnel can insure a 100 percent satisfaction level. However, it is possible to use insights and good procedures to increase the probability of choosing persons who will be satisfied, fulfilled, and productive in their work."[2] The qualities discussed here,

2. Introduction of unpublished summary of "Research Project for the Division for Service and Mission in America of The American Lutheran Church," phases two and three, prepared by the Midwest Career Development Service, 1975.

therefore, are not intended as a checklist. They are criteria, that, taken together, may serve as the basis for selecting a new church pastor.

The American Lutheran Church has recently developed a theoretical framework and criteria to distinguish effective new church pastors from less effective ones. The criteria center around managerial orientation and the ability to get things done. This model was tested to find those characteristics of pastors that could best predict which applicants for positions as mission pastors (new church pastors) would do the best job.

The project revealed fourteen items with high statistically significant predictive power: level of realism, ability to face problems directly, persuasiveness, optimism about the future of the church, capacity to utilize resources, enterprising (including managerial orientation and the ability to get things done), sensitivity to others' needs, positive outlook, self-starter, overall rating, ability to deal with one's own anger, aggressiveness, ability to analyze situations, and concern for evangelism.[3] Note the high correlation between these items and many of the characteristics listed earlier.

Role of the Judicatory

At the beginning of this chapter it was pointed out that one of the last main tasks of the person responsible for the processes leading up to the establishment of the new congregation is the selection of the first pastor. This does not mean that once the pastor has been chosen, the judicatory has no further responsibility. There is a wider support role on the part of the judicatory or denomination that continues until the new congregation is self-supporting and beyond. With regard to the pastor specifically, the judicatory should provide:

1. An adequate salary for a full-time pastor. Enough has already been said about the duties of the first pastor to

3. Ibid., p. 7.

show that he must give full attention to the new church. The pastor cannot be a student serving part time, a retired person giving a limited number of hours per week, or a person who must divide his time between the new congregation and pastoral responsibilities in other churches or ministries. A full-time minister with the qualities described above requires more than a minimum level salary. If a person with the proper credentials is to be interested in the job, an adequate salary must be offered.

2. An adequate parsonage or housing allowance. The unstable conditions associated with starting a new congregation must not be magnified or added to by expecting the pastor and his family to live in cramped or unusual quarters until the church can afford to provide adequate housing. This must be accomplished before the first pastor arrives. In many respects the parsonage will be the headquarters for the church during the first few weeks and months. Many meetings may be held there, and part of a back bedroom may serve as the first church office until an outside facility can be obtained. While the pastor and his family will be called upon to make sacrifices in this regard, more than this should not be expected or asked for.

3. A system of personal support. If the pastor is to provide the stability for the new congregation, who will assist him during times of dependency? The American Lutheran study cited above found that most new church pastors receive the greatest support from their spouses. Lay leaders ranked second, denominational executives were third, and peers came in a distant fourth. Perhaps this finding implies that spouses should be included in all orientation sessions for the pastor and some training events. But it may also imply that the bishop or judicatory official must take more responsibility for providing this support.

4. Evaluation and counsel. The judicatory executive, as part of his supervisory responsibilities, should periodically examine and evaluate the progress of the new congregation and the work of the pastor. The results of each evaluation, which may come as often as every six months for the first year and at least annually thereafter, should be shared

with the pastor and the appropriate committee of the church, and counsel offered where appropriate. The delicate task for the judicatory executive in this regard is allowing the pastor freedom to do his job without leaving him "alone." Except in unusual circumstances, the evaluation and counsel should be supportive rather than judgmental. The judicatory executive, however, must recognize his final responsibility to act quickly and decisively when glaring failures are discovered.

5. Training experiences. The judicatory can help the new church pastor with the cost of participating in training events and continuing education opportunities. These will be needed immediately and at various times to upgrade his skills in developing the new church. New pastors should also be urged to visit other new church pastors during the early weeks to learn from their experiences.

Tenure

If a pastor takes on the challenge and responsibility of developing a new congregation, how long should he be expected to remain at the church? A complementary question is, How can one tell whether the first pastor has stayed too long? There are no hard and fast rules.

If one of the primary roles of the pastor of a new church is that of giving the new congregation stability, however, it logically follows that the pastor should stay long enough for the church to attain stability in its new life. Generally a congregation of three hundred fifty to four hundred members or more with the first building unit in place is not dependent upon the pastor in the same way it was earlier. Often, therefore, it is good for the first pastor to remain until the new church at least reaches that membership, attains self-support, or occupies the first unit of its own building.

If the pastor remains into the intermediate stage of the church's development following its attainment of self-support, the church may be overly influenced by the person and possibly become so totally dependent upon him that there is a harmful and traumatic transitional period when a change is made. Also, pastors may get into a rut or become overly dependent on the congregation. Churches that grow rapidly and become successful quickly are the ones most likely to be faced with the problem of keeping a pastor too long or knowing when he should leave.

Perhaps an optimum time for the first pastor to stay in the "average" new church is five to seven years. There are few churches, new or old, whose pastors serve them as effectively after ten to twelve years or longer, as they did in their earlier years.

Other Professional and Supporting Staff

Ideally, every new church should have in addition to a pastor, a part-time director of music, a part-time secretary (if not a full-time one), and custodial and maintenance services by the time the first unit is completed. During the first year these services may be rendered by volunteers. But they are all duties that the pastor should not be expected to do and that should be contracted from paid professionals at the earliest possible date. In most cases, a person who is paid for his services will carry them out in a more professional manner. There are usually enough other less-demanding jobs that can be filled by volunteers. When volunteers are used for any of these tasks, they should not be asked to keep them indefinitely. A quarter, or two quarters at most, is long enough.

The new church may also do well to make use of outside consultants. As a new institution, the new congregation will have unique problems. In most cases consultants can be found with wide experience in such problem areas as organizational development, Christian education, building procedures, legal questions, use of small groups, and so on. They will have seen many similar situations and have some solutions to this new church's problems. Often they can be secured from denominational and judicatory staffs, other churches (in the same or another denomination), or outside organizations.

11 : Gathering and Organizing the New Congregation

Ideally, when the pastor arrives on the scene, he or she has a community to serve, the results of a community survey that is now no more than one year old (hopefully less), financial backing, a mission design, and a mandate to organize a new congregation. Where does he begin?

Learning the Community

He begins by getting to know the area (metropolitan area, city, or county) and the local community. Using the general area survey, the feasibility study, an automobile, and a guide who is familiar with the area, he begins to make a windshield survey of the larger arena in which he will serve. He gets to know major thoroughfares, the location of hospitals and institutions, other churches, shopping centers, and differences in residential areas.

He may talk with community business people, leaders in city and area government, community professionals, workers in social service, welfare, and other person-centered programs, and the principals and teachers in the schools. In other words, the new pastor needs to talk to many of the same people who were interviewed at the time of the general area survey or feasibility study. But, he talks with them for a different purpose. His purpose is to get to know the city and its people, and to have them know

119

him, like him, and support him as he attempts to develop a new community institution. Through this communication and looking at the city, he gets to know the area geographically, ecologically, socially, economically, and politically.

The new pastor should then spend several days or weeks getting to know the community for which he has special responsibility. He should check out the data behind the feasibility study and update them as he goes about his work. He can talk with many people locally and even in surrounding communities about the particular needs of the people, the special opportunities and limitations in the community, and how a church can be structured to make their lives full and whole. Again, the pastor should talk to as many people as possible regardless of their past or present religious affiliation, He cannot decide the kind of church that the community needs. It is his job to be a sounding board for the people so they may help him structure the kind of religious community that is needed.

L. Floyd Carmack, pastor of the Bonanza United Church of Christ in Jonesboro, Georgia, recently wrote in a denominational publication about his style of ministry. He said:

> I began my ministry in Bonanza in September of 1966. I felt that my first job was to get to know the people and have them get to know me. I visited every home in Bonanza, which at that time was about 77 . . . . I feel that the success or failure of any new church start will depend on the minister getting to know the community. He or she should be involved in the community. His first purpose there is to make known his Christ. In order to do this, he has to be willing to visit and counsel with anyone and everyone without regard to whether they come to his church or not.[1]

By the end of the first few weeks, the pastor should begin to feel that he is part of the community he has been

1. *NCD Potpourri*, December, 1974, p. 15.

called to serve. He will have met a lot of people and learned a lot of history and interesting folklore about the area and the community.

Community Visitation

Through the use of the community survey cards prepared as part of the feasibility study before his coming, the pastor can begin to visit in the homes of people who indicated an interest in starting a new church of that denomination. As he visits, he can update the census in each neighborhood, going back to houses where no one was contacted and visiting new families who have moved in. He should use every available means to learn of people who might be interested in the new church.

Before beginning the concentrated visitation program, the pastor should prepare a brochure that introduces the new church. This brochure is a publicity piece that the pastor can distribute as he visits in homes. Since he and his family are the only visible part of the new church so far, the brochure introduces them, perhaps with a family photograph. It tells about the type of new church expected, the community it will serve, the reason a new church is needed, and the schedule of major events during the first year (including the date, time, and place of the first worship service, the first church school session, the service of constitution, etc.). It should extend an invitation to participate and give in bold letters the address and telephone number where the new pastor can be reached. The brochure may contain a small map showing the location of the site on which the new church building will be erected.

As the minister calls in the community, his concern is to gather a congregation. He is looking for a core group. It may be that no one from the community has been contacted or has participated in the planning for the new church. One would hope this is not the case and that many residents have participated. Sometimes members of churches in other communities who now live in this one have been recruited to help establish the church. They may be people who expect to be members of the new church, or people who want to work with it during the first few months.

As the new pastor goes about gathering and organizing the new institution, procedures and methods that have been used successfully in the past may be of some value. The procedures outlined in this chapter, it should be understood, should not be seen as "helpful hints that will guarantee success." They are suggested as one way to proceed at various points, not *the* only way. They may be most helpful and appropriate for the more traditionally gathered congregations.

Gathering the Members

As the pastor goes about calling in the neighborhood, he can develop a list of the families who have indicated interest. This list should include the names of persons who expressed interest during the survey, as well as people in the community suggested by other churches of his denomination and all other sources. This becomes the constituency list from which many will become members. It will continually expand and perhaps be the most important document the church has during its first year.

In the initial stages, most of the calling is done by the pastor. As lay people become committed to the new church, they too will find and gather interested people. Remember that the purpose of this calling program is both to share information about the church's plans and to listen to the people talk about their concerns for the community and what they would like to see in a new church. It is important that people who are invited to participate be given an early opportunity to express their ideas about the nature and style of the new congregation.

From the list of families on the constituency list and other sources, a mailing list needs to be made. At the beginning this list should be as inclusive as possible. It may include people who have not expressed interest in this church but are not now involved in a church and have indicated that they may become involved in the future. As people indicate that they have no interest in the church, their names can be removed from the list. New names should be added daily or weekly. By the third month, it is essential to begin a twice monthly mailing to interested people, keeping them up to date on the progress and new plans of the church. The pastor cannot continue to go back and visit in the homes of prospects but neither can he afford to wait several months before communicating with them after his first visit. This list gives him an opportunity to stay in touch with the growing constituency.

INTEREST MEETINGS

When the number of interested families reaches twenty-five to thirty-five, or by the end of the second month, the pastor should divide them into groups of eight, ten, or twelve families and ask a "key" family to host each group in an informal meeting in their home to discuss the new church. The key families should be people who have expressed interest in the new church, are known in the community, have some leadership ability, are willing to serve on a planning committee for the new congregation for the first few critical months, and are willing to host the small group meetings in their homes. The pastor should send a written invitation to each family in the congregation to attend a particular small group meeting, with the host family following up with a personal telephone invitation several days before the event. People who cannot attend one meeting may be invited to attend another at a more convenient time. It is important that the pastor schedule his activities so that he can be present at each of the small group meetings.

The purpose of the small groups is for people to get better acquainted with each other and discuss their concerns about the new church. The pastor should be prepared to ask a series of questions to get the discussion going and keep it going. For example: What style of congregation is needed in this community? What type of worship service will be most helpful to you? What facets of the church program should have the most emphasis? What experiences with the church have been most meaningful to you in the past? How would you be willing to serve in the new church if called upon?

Organizing the Congregation

Following the small group meetings, the key families should meet as a planning committee. Each person should share in a general discussion the findings of the small group meetings.

The planning group must begin to study and discuss the preliminary mission design for the congregation. They should think about their own goals for the church in relation to it and begin to construct their own statement of mission. The final mission design may not be completed for several months.

The planning committee will also make plans for the first worship service and first church school session. It is probably best to divide the group into task forces to work on specific plans. The group should serve as the coordinating committee until the church is formally constituted.

THE FIRST WORSHIP SERVICE

Many times the new pastor, as soon as he arrives, discovers that the first worship service has already been scheduled for the following Sunday. Or he may schedule one himself within the first couple of weeks. In either case he must frantically find people to attend that service without first getting to know the community or having an opportunity to structure a meaningful worship service. It is very important that the first worship service should not be held until all of the steps discussed above have been taken, which usually means that it will be two or three months or more after the pastor arrives. If this first worship service is meaningful and well attended, the new church will be off to a good start. If not, it may have a depressing effect. Representatives of nearby churches and the judicatory may be invited to attend the service.

The first service should be a family worship service for school-age children and older. A nursery should be provided for younger children at all worship services. Many churches have found that it is helpful to give a name tag to all worshipers as they arrive and an invitation to a coffee-fellowship period following the service. While others may be invited to assist, it is important that the pastor conduct the service and preach the first sermon. The people in the community are not concerned about the history of the congregation at this point and do not want long speeches from outsiders. They want to hear and evaluate the leadership ability and preaching talents of the local pastor.

USING THE MEDIA

Churches are notorious in their lack of use of the communications media to advertise significant events. Many retail stores would be out of business if they were as lax as churches. The event of the first worship service is one that should be advertised broadly. Ads may be taken in newspapers, and radio spots should be requested or bought. Brochures and posters may be placed in community commercial establishments. Word of mouth is the most important method of advertisement for the new church, but it should not be the only one. Particularly if the community is growing very rapidly, it is the church's responsibility to see that each new family knows that there is a new church of this denomination already started (or about to start), where it is meeting, and at what time.

THE CHURCH SCHOOL

The first church school session should be held at least one or two weeks after the first worship service. Since all the people are in unfamiliar surroundings and often in a building that was not designed for use as a church, to have both a church school session and worship service on the first Sunday can be confusing.

Before starting the church school the pastor and planning committee should seriously consider the best time of the week to have it. If the church is meeting in a place that does not lend itself well to church school activities, it may be best scheduled for a weekday afternoon for the children, or for the whole family on a weekday evening. This will be appropriate for churches in some communities but not for others.

The church school teaching staff should be asked to serve for only three months. Some of the people who take on this responsibility will not be trained for the task or have experience in doing it. At the end of the first three months, the teachers and the responsible planning committee will be free to suggest changes in the make-up of classes and their leadership.

TEMPORARY TREASURER

A temporary treasurer should be selected by the planning committee before the first worship service. This person should be bonded and should open a bank account in the name of "The New (denominational name) Church," so that the people at the first worship service can be informed that it is possible to make a check payable to the church and that offerings will be taken at each service.

NEW MEMBERS

It is well to plan for the first group of new members to indicate their wish to join at the third or fourth worship service. Some denominations do not allow a pastor to receive the new members until the church is constituted. Persons wishing to join the new church before the service of constitution can make this desire known publicly and take the vows of membership, even though the membership will not be fully consummated or confirmed until the constitution service. When this is explained to new mom bers ahead of time, it creates no real problems. In some denominations the members of a new church before constitution are members of the judicatory.

MEMBERSHIP TRAINING

Membership training experiences will vary by denomination, and by congregation and pastor in some denominations. Perhaps everything that is done in the new church in the initial months should be considered a part of the total membership training experience. Specific training events should be provided for persons received into the church on profession of faith or persons transferring from other denominations. Separate sessions may be held for youth, or they may be held for entire families. People who have not been members of the denomination before must have the opportunity to learn the doctrines and polity of the church.

THE SERVICE OF CONSTITUTION

The service of constitution is the point at which the people who have been meeting together in worship, study, and planning groups officially become a church. It is at this point that they say to the community, "We are now a fellowship of believers in Jesus Christ who have established a social institution for the purpose of worship, prayer, nurture, and service. Everyone who will may come."

In most denominations a service of constitution is required by church law. In addition to being required in most churches, the service of constitution has other benefits for the congregation. It allows for and demands that this group of people have self-determination. They are no longer dependent upon another church or the larger denomination. It is a taking on of responsibility and a new freedom. It allows this congregation to decide what Christ calls it to be in this community.

When a congregation should hold the service of constitution varies. Sometimes it is held from three to six months after the first worship service. Many churches feel that it is best to wait until it can be expected that the new church (particularly a neighborhood or metropolitan-regional one) will have eighty to one hundred charter members. To charter with less than that number may damage the church's image, and the church may find itself with too few members to carry out all of the responsibilities placed upon it. Usually the church should be constituted by the end of the first year.

Most denominations have a suggested order of service for the constituting or chartering of a new church. Some congregations make their own, which is probably good discipline and gives the church the opportunity to express their identity in the community. In addition to hymns, prayers, litanies, reading of the Scripture, and sermon, the service may also include a declaration of purpose, confirmation of charter members with presentation of certificates, confirmation of the organization by the judicatory administrator, and a united response by the congregation accepting the responsibility of being a church.

Generally, the name of the new church will have been decided upon, and the church will be officially named at the constitution service. It should be selected by the local congregation in consultation with the judicatory administrator. The name can be very important for the new church; it should be chosen deliberately and in a democratic manner by the early members.

ELECTION OF OFFICERS

A slate of officers for the church should be presented to the newly formed congregation for election at or just following the service of constitution. A nominating committee composed of persons who have publicly made it known that they intend to join the new church should make the nominations. The pastor should be chairman.

The number of church officers and the positions they will fill vary from denomination to denomination according to church law. Generally the following officers are elected:

1. The official administrative board, which has oversight over all activities in the church.

2. A program planning committee.

3. A board of trustees.

4. A treasurer and financial secretary. This probably will be the same person for the first year.

5. A lay leader or representative to represent the laity of the church as needed, particularly on judicatory and denominational committees.

6. Others as required by church law or deemed necessary by the particular congregation.

The structure for the new church should be kept to a minimum. Also, the number in each of the official boards and committees should be kept small so that others may be added as new members are received into the church. Often a small group is more functional than a larger one. As the church becomes larger, however, representation will be as important as function.

The pastor should write a brief job description for each of the offices to which people are to be nominated. Many of the people who fill these jobs have not been members of a church before or of a church of this denomination. They need to have in writing what will be expected of them.

The Larger Task

Soon after the service of constitution, a combined meeting should be held of the three primary groups elected— the official administrative board, the program planning committee, and the board of trustees. At this meeting the preliminary mission design and official denominational handbooks should be used to determine the responsibilities of the congregation and particularly the specific responsibilities of each of these three groups. By discussing them together, each group will know the larger task, their own, and those of other groups in the church.

This group should again review the mission design, perhaps apportioning parts of it to each of the three groups for detailed review and development. Each group may add goals and strategies in its area of responsibility. It is important that a revised mission design be completed, although not finalized, at specific points over the following months so that it can be shared with the congregation and receive their input.

One of the officially elected groups, for example, may have the responsibility of revising or writing a statement of mission that will capsule the primary aims and tasks of the new church. The statement should be brief but clear and distinctive for this congregation. It should not be copied in whole or in part from that of another congregation. The initial draft by the small group should then be submitted as is, or with the rest of the mission design, to the entire congregation for additions and further work.

12 : Planning and Financing a Building

Need for a Place

Whether or not to have a permanent building is not an issue in most new congregations.[1] While some congregations in the past quarter century have done without physical space for their activities and have sought to operate unencumbered by buildings or walls, few of these churches have survived more than a decade. Even those churches that have survived without their own buildings have for the most part resorted to using existing community buildings or to renting or sharing space with another congregation. Such congregations cannot be called "churches without walls." They are merely using someone else's walls.

All congregations need a "place" (physical structure of some kind) that can serve as a tangible focal point, as well as provide a facility in which to gather and call new members. Some special purpose congregations that remain very small by design may not need their own permanent building. This will be particularly true of style-centered congre-

1. Parts of this chapter are adapted from *The Church Building Process*, by H. Paul Smith and Ezra Earl Jones. It is a detailed guide for any church planning to build. Copies may be obtained through the church extension offices of most denominations.

gations that want to meet in homes or can arrange to rent space on a continuing basis. Most congregations, however, will want and need their own buildings.

New neighborhood and open country churches, and some churches of other types, may find it possible and even advisable to plan and build permanent multipurpose facilities. These buildings should be designed so that worship, education, recreation, fellowship, administration, and service programs can all be adequately housed in the same space at different times of the day or week. A wide variety of church furnishings are now available that are attractive, portable, easily stacked and stored, and appropriate for a wide variety of functions.

Most new metropolitan-regional, downtown, and small town churches will still need multiunit facilities. Many of these facilities consist of three basic units—worship center (sanctuary), educational building, and fellowship hall. One would hope that such churches will not plan facilities without giving careful thought to their appropriateness for their own congregation. One or another type may not be needed by some churches.

Shared Facilities

Sometimes congregations of different denominations in a new community consider constructing one building that can be used by both congregations. This strategy may be considered more and more in the future as building costs increase, but caution is advised until better models are provided. If the two congregations are similar in theology, polity, and activities, they may want to use the building at the same times, thus requiring a compromise that is really acceptable to neither. The shared-facilities concept may work better with churches that are quite different; for example, a United Methodist church sharing space with a Seventh-Day Adventist church, or a Roman Catholic congregation with a Presbyterian church.

Initial Facilities

The first "headquarters" of the new church may be the den or a spare room in the pastor's home, loaned or rented office space in a nearby church or community facility, or the garage of a neighbor. From this "makeshift office," equipped with no more than a telephone, table, chair, and a few supplies, the pastor carries out the initial task of making contacts in the community and communicating information about the new congregation.

Larger facilities will be needed by the time the first worship service is held. Space may be rented from or loaned by a school, country club, community center, or another church. Mobile or portable buildings can often be erected on the church's site and used until permanent facilities are provided. The denomination or judicatory may own such buildings for use by new congregations. If not, the new congregation may purchase them with the plan that (1) they may be used even after the first unit of the permanent building is built, or (2) they can be sold for other uses when they are no longer needed.

In other situations a nearby abandoned church building or other unused facility in the community can provide a home for the congregation until permanent arrangements are made. Occasionally, judicatories have had permanent first units constructed before the congregation was gathered. While this is handy to the new church during the first year, it is not recommended. Often such buildings later prove to be too small. Permanent facilities should reflect the corporate life of the congregation, its distinctive needs and program. Building the structure first decreases the church's flexibility in planning its own mission design and style of ministry.

One of the best methods is to acquire a temporary building that is placed on the church's permanent site. The church then has an early visible and tangible image in the community. People acknowledge its existence and watch its progress. They feel that such a church has more permanence and stability than one meeting in a rented facility that is also used for other activities.

Use of an abandoned church or rented facility is also an acceptable alternative. An abandoned church building must be in or very near the community to be served. A lot of energy can be expended in rearranging and preparing for each activity in a rented facility, but a willing committee of people can often be recruited for the task. The danger of using temporary facilities, as churches in Starkville, Mississippi, and Winston Salem, North Carolina, can attest, is that the congregation tends to depend on them too long and not feel pushed to provide permanent facilities in a reasonable length of time. When this happens, the church again seems temporary. Some residents may delay affiliation until permanency is assured. Generally, if a permanent building is to be constructed, it should be started by the beginning of the church's third year.

Factors Affecting Future Buildings

Regardless of the type and size of buildings needed, two crucial components of all future decisions concerning buildings will be availability of building materials and cost. In some areas of the country, certain basic building materials have been in short supply for several years, and scattered, if not widespread, shortages will probably become routine in the future.

The cost of both materials and labor has increased steadily while church membership has leveled off and declined in many areas. Church budgets have held stable or increased slightly in the main but at much slower rates than inflation and building costs. There is an increasing need for keeping both the number and size of buildings to a minimum. The rising cost of land and the decreasing availability of energy will join with high construction costs to make this imperative. Now, as never before, proper planning and adequate supervision at critical stages in the building process are necessary to achieve architectural beauty and quality construction at a reasonable cost.

Preliminary Planning

Whether to build should be decided by a carefully selected committee after a thorough study of the church, its program, and goals to determine the type and amount of space needed for the various activities of the congregation. This committee should also decide in the preliminary planning process what is needed, when, and how much should be built as a part of the first unit. The process should include two time frames: (1) the first five to eight years of the congregation's life; and (2) nine to ten years and beyond.

Preliminary planning is not the design stage of development. It is simply looking at needs and resources with regard to worship, education, fellowship, administration, and finance.

Long-range Planning Committee

The preliminary study and planning function should be assigned to a special task force: the "long-range planning committee," the "program survey committee," or some similar committee. The distinction here is that the initial planning committee is concerned with generalized evaluation, program analysis, and the type and amount of space needed by this particular congregation. The building committee, which will begin to function later, will have a narrowly defined task related to construction procedures.

The long-range planning committee should be composed of a representative cross section of the congregation. It is important that all program activities be adequately represented to assure that no function is overlooked in the evaluation and that the needs for all types of building space or equipment are considered.

The committee should plan on the basis of ideals. However, as it does so, it must always be aware that limited resources may make it impossible to realize the ideal. In spite of such limitations, a better job will be done if ideals are scaled down later to fit resources, rather than plans being made from the outset according to their feasibility. Consideration of the church's resources—persons and money—can be introduced into the process after all needs and opportunities have been discussed.

Need for an Architect

No building program of significance should be attempted without the services of a competent architect. Frequently churches ask, "Why don't we save the architect's fee by allowing a contractor to design our building and have members of the congregation supervise construction?" The answer is simply that you will not "save" the architect's fee. The mistakes that are made without such professional advice and service cost far more than the fee involved. Not only are many planning and design mistakes avoided, but a competent architect can suggest use of new materials and construction techniques that are not familiar to amateurs. These alone result in significant savings. In terms of money saved, funds used for architectural services are the best spent on the project.

Selection of the Architect

One of the best ways to judge an architect's ability is to examine buildings he or she has designed. Take time to observe and study existing church buildings that have been constructed in recent years. Secure the names of the architects who designed them. Then, schedule interviews with representatives of the congregations who have worked with the architect. In the interview, try to determine:

1. Was the relationship a satisfactory one?
2. Was the architect able to give sympathetic hearing to your specific problems?
3. Did he provide creative solutions to design problems?
4. Was his relationship to the contractor or builders harmonious?

This process will enable the committee to compile a list of several architects who appear to merit consideration and, ultimately, to select the one to be employed.

In the selection of an architect for a racial or ethnic congregation, it is imperative that the architect appreciate the unique cultural traditions of the group. He must also understand their distinctive patterns of church life and programming. Sometimes the person may be of the ethnic group himself. When that is not possible, he should display a willingness to learn.

Before a contract is executed between the church and an architect, the church must have a clear understanding of the importance of providing essential information to him. The notion that the selection of an architect frees the congregation of all future work is extremely fallacious. The architect is an agent of the church whose skills are indispensable. However, he must know what the church needs before he can create a design for it. The question of need must be answered by the church through its planning committee. When this need has been clearly identified, work on the proposed design can begin.

The Architect and the Building Budget

Not only must the church define the function, it must give the architect a specific budget figure for the project. Of course, it is unrealistic to expect him to guarantee that the bids received will match the budget figure. However, a maximum cost has to be established. A contigency item of an additional 5 to 10 percent can be added for protection against high bids as the architect's estimate can be 10 percent high or low and be considered acceptable. If the low bid goes significantly higher, the contract with the architect should obligate him to do the necessary redesign work to bring the cost within the budget figure without obligating the church to pay an additional architectural fee.

Without a budget ceiling, extreme disappointments may occur. Picture this scene: A congregation has proceeded into the design and specification stage without ever giving the architect a budget figure. The plans have been finalized and submitted to the church, approval has been given, and the work accepted. The bids are 40 to 50 percent higher than expected. The church cannot possibly proceed with construction, and yet it has a set of drawings and specifications on hand. The architect has submitted these in good faith, and the church has accepted them. The fact that the congregation cannot afford to build is not the architect's fault. He has a right to submit a bill for services based upon a percentage of the lowest bid. If the bids are so high that it is necessary to do a complete redesign, the church is obligated to pay an architectural design fee for the second time. All of this can be avoided by establishing a budget before the architect is commissioned.

The following items must be a part of the expected costs of the project: basic construction; site purchase and development (if needed); landscaping; parking area; electrical, water, and sewer services; architect's fee; furnishings and equipment; legal fees; insurance (builder's risk); performance bond; interest charges for construction money; and any existing indebtedness that must be refinanced.

It should be emphasized that the total of the above must be an estimate, not a "guesstimate." While an estimate is never a firm figure, it is possible to achieve a reasonable degree of accuracy. Architects and builders have up-to-date information on building costs at any given time. They can provide a range of square-foot averages for various types of construction. With this information, it is possible to assign a probable cost to the basic construction. Once the scope of site development and landscaping has been determined, a cost estimate can easily be made. The manufacturers of furnishings and equipment can provide prices for all of these items and sometimes will give firm proposals. This makes it unnecessary to proceed on the basis of vague guessing. To estimate probable interest charges for construction financing (money borrowed to pay construction costs), it can be assumed that it will be roughly equal to the interest on the full amount of the loan for one-half of the time of construction. In other words, if construction is expected to take a year, calculate the interest on a six-month period. Funds will have been disbursed on a month-by-month basis and interest will be charged only on money actually disbursed.

Building Fund Potential

An immediate question that must be faced in the development of a financial plan is, How much do we expect to raise ourselves? Obviously, there are significant variations among congregations. In an average church it ought to be possible to raise within a three-year pledge period an amount equal to twice the annual current operations budget. Some congregations raise more than this. Other denominations have found that their churches seldom raise more than one and one-half times the annual budget. When estimating the probable average monthly receipts on building fund pledges, discount them a minimum of 10 percent. It is better to budget on a conservative basis than to assume 100 percent performance.

Fund-raising Counsel

During the past twenty years an increasing number of congregations have employed professional fund raisers to secure building capital. In general this approach has been successful, and many congregations have even employed the same people and methods for current operations budgets.

Fund raising is a special task, which can best be accomplished by the application of special skills. Seldom are such skills available within the congregation, and when they are, it is likely that the people with these skills do not have time to assume this additional responsibility. Many pastors possess some skill in this area, but in general it is best that they not use it in their own congregations. To do so is to try to function in two full-time roles, and overall efficiency is sacrificed.

It is not unusual to hear a church member say, "Let's do it ourselves and save all that money that we would have to pay for professional help." The fallacy is that you do not "save that money"; you simply do not have it to save. This proposal assumes that unaided effort produces the same results that would be obtained with professional help. It just is not so. Experience has shown that the average congregation will raise from 20 to 30 percent more by using professional counsel than it will through its own unaided effort. If counsel is available through the denomination, the cost seldom exceeds 2.5 percent of the total amount raised and is considerably less in some denominations. Commercial organizations may charge from 5 to 10 percent. It is apparent that the additional amount raised and the savings in interest cost on borrowed funds is well worth the cost of the consultant.

The Master Building Plan

Some churches, particularly those which plan one-stage, multiple-purpose facilities, will not need a master plan. Churches that expect to build additional facilities later should draw a master plan before anything else is done. An acceptable plan ensures that when the first unit is built, it will bear a reasonable relation to all possible future units so that in the years to come each increment will fit into a harmonious whole, and the total completed structure will provide all the needed facilities. The master plan should deal primarily with traffic patterns within the building, orientation on the site, parking facilities, the relation of one functional unit to another, overall style, and the facilities that will be needed at various stages of development of the congregation.

The original master plan need not be considered as the absolute final solution. In fact, it is likely that substantial changes will be made later. Experience with the first unit and changes within the congregation itself may dictate changes in future development. However, the original master plan does represent one acceptable solution to the design problem.

Since it is impossible to draw up this master plan without an architect, the church should expect to pay for this service. It is best to consider this expense as a separate item in the building budget. The contract with the architect may specify his responsibility to develop the master plan, but the congregation should not obligate itself to the architect for the detailed design of future buildings. Pay him for the master plan, contract for the design of the first unit if desired, and leave the balance for negotiation at a later time.

The Building Committee

The function of the building committee differs from that of the long-range planning committee. Both committees are concerned with building, but long-range planning has to do with overall strategy, development, and programming. The building committee takes over to implement the construction after the decision has been made to proceed. In effect, the building committee is called upon to function as an executive arm of the long-range planning committee and the congregation.

The building committee must be sensitive to the opinion of the congregation. The congregation will have had opportunity to participate in the planning done by the long-range planning committee, and the building committee must review the report of this committee. However, as construction gets under way, the committee at times should seek advice from other members of the congregation. Although the building committee should be few in number, it must never be "closed." When any part of the congregation feels that the committee is unresponsive, the building program is apt to be in trouble.

The first activity of the building committee is to assist the architect in the preparation of preliminary plans. These plans will be approved by the congregation before any further steps are taken. The importance of preliminary plans lies in their use as the basis of detailed planning. Planning and design errors should be detected and appropriate revisions made while the plans are still in a preliminary form. Changes in preliminary drawings are not expensive. At this stage changes are merely lines on paper. However, if errors are not detected until final working drawings and specifications have been completed, the cost of changes may be very high. If errors go undetected until the building is under construction, it may be difficult to make corrections without involving unacceptable costs. Many hours of the architect's time will have gone into working drawings. Changes at that stage cannot be made without adequate compensation, especially if the church formally approved the preliminary plans.

When the preliminary plans have been approved, the committee can proceed with a realistic estimate of cost. This may lead to revision of the plan—either expansion or contraction. In any event, the preliminary plan indicates the size, the style, and the material composition of the structure, and these must be known before a cost estimate can be made. It is still only an estimate, but if it is done carefully, it can give a good indication of the ability of the church to proceed and be the basis for a loan request.

If cost estimates indicate that the building project can be undertaken, the committee may authorize the architect to begin preparation of detailed plans and specifications. When completed, the plans should be approved by the governing body of the church.

Selection of the First Unit for Construction

New congregations that will need more than one building unit do not usually have the money to construct the entire church plant at one time. Thus the church must choose which part is to have priority.

For the average churchgoer the emotional attachment to sanctuary-oriented worship is so great that many new congregations consider building the worship center prior to any other unit. To do this is usually a mistake. The construction of the worship center as the first unit consumes all available resources of the congregation. Moreover, it is essentially a single-purpose facility—for corporate worship. Because of financial considerations, several years are likely to elapse before the congregation can build the second unit. The ultimate growth of the congregation, however, depends in part upon having facilities for educational and fellowship activities. Since all of the money and energy will have gone into the construction of a worship center, the growth of the congregation is likely to be impaired by the absence of adequate educational and fellowship facilities. In many instances congregations that decide to build the worship center as the first unit never need any other.

If the master plan consists of three basic units (educational building, fellowship hall, and worship center) and only one can be constructed initially, it generally should be the fellowship hall. If properly designed, it can accommodate, at least in a limited way, all the functions of the congregation until a second unit can be built.

The construction of a fellowship hall that can house all of the functions of the new or relocated congregation presents a challenging problem. The building must provide flexibility for use in the initial stages, but fit harmoniously into an ultimate master plan. This can be done if the church and the architect spend the necessary time in the study of its use. All decisions must take into account not only the current need but the ultimate use of the structure when all other units have been built.

Selection of the Contractor

A contractor may be selected by the church and the construction cost agreed upon by negotiation. However, this is not the most common practice. If the cost of the job is significant, the church should seek competitive bids from general contractors. The architect prepares the necessary drawings and specifications and submits these to contractors for bids. A specific date is announced for the submission of sealed bids, and the architect presides at the bid openings.

The bid invitation should clearly specify that the church reserves the right to reject any and all bids. Although it may seek competitive bids, it is not obligated to accept the lowest, and it can limit the number it will receive. This is done by having the architect announce that bidding is by invitation.

If the congregation has a building contractor in its membership, he may ask to submit a bid. In general it is poor policy to award contracts to a member. The main objection is that the positions of both the church and the contractor are compromised. Because he is a member of the congregation, the church may expect him to give it certain advantages that it would not otherwise receive. This is not fair to him. On the other hand, if he encounters difficulty in discharging his contract obligations, he may expect considerations from the church that he would not receive on another job. This is unfair to the church.

When it is necessary for a church to borrow money to finance construction, the lender will usually require the contractor to submit a performance bond. Even if not required by the lender, it is still a good policy and is recommended. Churches frequently resist paying a bond premium because they think the requirement for a bond questions the integrity of the contractor. This is not so. There may be any number of reasons for failure to perform a contract. In one situation a church was only one-half built when the contractor died unexpectedly leaving no one to carry on his business. The roof was not in place at the time, and extensive weather damage occurred during the long months of court litigation and searching for another builder. If the church had secured a performance bond, the bonding company would have assured completion.

Borrowing

Several denominations have special funds or foundations from which loans are made available to local churches for buildings. Ordinarily, the terms a church receives from a denominational fund are comparable to those offered by a local bank. Sometimes, though, the interest rate through the denomination is lower. One of the primary contributions of denominational funds is that loans can be made at the standard rate or a reduced rate to small minority or special purpose churches that would not be eligible for conventional bank loans. In some denominations reduced interest rates are available to any new congregation.

The most conventional form of church borrowing is the customary bank mortgage loan secured by a first lien on the church property. If this is the source of funding, then the rules are very well established, and the major decision to be made by the church has to do with the availability of loans and the terms. Although there is nothing especially complicated about the rules governing such a loan, the amount to be borrowed is of major importance to the life of the church. A mistake at this point may result in the failure of the church in future years. Few things are as destructive to congregational morale and effectiveness as excessive indebtedness.

Excessive indebtedness is not a problem that can be easily solved. Since mortgage obligations are priority items in the budget, programs are likely to be undersupported. Whenever the debt-servicing item is so great that it impairs the program of the church, it is too high. The church exists for more profound purposes than paying off a real estate mortgage. *In general no church should borrow an amount which requires more than one-third of its total annual income for amortization purposes.* Experience throughout the Church indicates that difficulty can be anticipated if this figure is appreciably exceeded.

Church Bond Issues

A bond issue is simply another form of indebtedness. It is neither good nor bad in itself, and the distinctive characteristics of each church bond program will determine this. The same principles that apply to a sound bank loan should also apply to a bond indebtedness. If the congregation incurs excessive indebtedness, the results are the same whether it is a bank loan or a bond issue.

It is easier to become excessively indebted through a bond issue than through the conventional bank loan. A bank or other lender will give close attention to the ability of the church to repay. The emphasis is on past performance and probable future resources. In a bond issue the maximum indebtedness may easily become the total of the bonds that can be sold. This could well be greatly in excess of the amount that the church can repay. In some instances, bonding companies may exercise responsible restraint; but in others "the sky is the limit."

Some bonding programs are tailored for sale to church boards rather than responsible financial counsel. The result is the introduction of propositions that are quite unrealistic. The most common is the notion that the construction of a building will promote congregational growth. Therefore, it is assumed that the church may be expected to carry a heavier debt reduction schedule in future years. This notion is used to justify an escalating payback schedule for bond retirement. Usually the "step-up" is timed for the third and fifth years of the program. If the church does not grow as projected, it is soon in financial trouble. Far too often churches have experienced difficulty in meeting the original schedule before even the first escalation occurs.

13 : Old Churches Can Become New

We recently wrote to 550 judicatory executives announcing a training event for pastors of new congregations and inviting the executives to submit the names of people who should participate. The response was diverse. Most of those who responded suggested persons who are engaged in developing congregations that have not existed before in new or rebuilt communities. It is these churches, which have been organized *de novo* (out of nothing), on which our discussion in this book has centered.

But many of the judicatory officers interpreted "new congregations" in other ways. For the most part they offered pastors' names who are serving congregations that have existed for many years, but that now must be "renewed" if they are to continue, or churches that have recently made or been forced to make a dramatic shift in emphasis, structure, or location that will result in their becoming significantly different institutions. In other words the attempt is being made to develop new churches on the base of existing ones.

A number of different situations were recounted. There was a church that recently relocated from an inner-urban neighborhood to the edge of the city; a downtown congregation that merged with a nearby neighborhood church; a small formerly rural church now caught in suburban transition; a formerly white church in a mostly black community that is trying to become a black church; a church started five years ago that has only eighty members and is attempting to start over with a new pastor; a church that declined from five hundred to two hundred members in recent years due to social class change in the community and wants to change its image and the thrust of its ministry.

While the establishment of congregations that have not existed before is assuming increased importance and is the major thrust of this book, we must acknowledge that renewal of present churches is an equally important concern, presently requires more attention by judicatory administrators and local church members, is imminently critical to our present Christian witness and mission (as well as that of the future), and must be approached in relation to and as a part of our total new church development efforts. As older churches recognize that they have lost their constituency, see another group of people who can be served, and attempt to become "new churches"— with new life, new challenge, new people, new facilities, new purpose, and/or a new style—the Church extends its ministry and is renewed itself in the process.

An Alternate Method

The definition of a new congregation introduced in chapter 1 and used throughout this volume includes the possibility of developing new churches from existing ones and merits our purposeful consideration here as an alternate method. In reality all forms of new congregations are commonly developed with people or resources from an existing congregation. Of course, churches are always related to other churches through transfer of members, but sometimes a block of people leave a large church to become the nucleus of a new suburban congregation. Selected individuals may be recruited from a church to lead in the creation of a mission congregation, or a church may be reconstituted as a mission with a new constituency when its former members have left and there are not enough to continue it as a self-supporting church. A new church in a redeveloped community may occupy a used church building or build on the site of a former church retained by the denomination for that purpose. Style-centered congregations are sometimes formed as fringe groups break away from established churches. Or an ecumenical congregation may be formed as the result of the union or federation of two or more churches of different denominations.

Racial and ethnic congregations have been primarily developed on the base of existing churches. This is particularly true for black congregations in urban areas, but it holds for Hispanics, Asians, and other groups as well. As a racial or ethnic group moved into inner-urban neighborhoods originally populated by whites or others, they either joined the churches that were there and eventually became the dominant group, or used buildings abandoned by the former residents to establish their own congregations. This method has created some problems for the minorities, particularly with regard to the old buildings, but it will likely continue to be one major strategy in minority new church development.

The need and appropriate methods for providing churches for racial and ethnic groups in the future depends in large measure on whether the present impetus for separate social institutions continues or whether inclusiveness becomes the goal. Based upon the rate and degree to which blacks and other nonwhites have been integrated into the mainstream of our society and its institutions in the past, and the additional factor of different languages for some groups, the former seems more realistic. Even if inclusiveness is once again claimed as the ultimate goal, segregated housing patterns and recognition of diversity in styles of worship and ministry will mean that some congregations specifically for racial and ethnic groups will be needed.

Perhaps it is most appropriate to say that racial and ethnic people will need churches developed by a variety of methods. In communities that are truly integrated, churches which reflect that quality can be created. It will be incumbent on the majority group to enable it to happen, however. In new communities developed initially by an ethnic group, totally new congregations as described in the preceding chapters of this book will be needed. Where the minority people are latecomers to an area, the new group may join existing churches, form new ones with no relationship to those already there, or work with the members of the churches that remain to provide for a transition to "new" congregations that reflect the character of the community and the religious needs of the people.

Redevelopment through a Comprehensive Strategy

The renewal of existing churches affects our efforts in new church development just as the new congregations have impact on existing churches. Both types of development must be seen as part of a comprehensive metropolitan or judicatory strategy.

To be painfully realistic, we must admit that few judicatories have done area surveys and developed strategies through which each local church can understand itself and its relationship to other congregations and the larger community. Most changes in congregations occur in response to an immediate problem or crisis. The problem is acute by the time it is given attention, and there is no time or energy then to deal with a larger strategy. Judicatory executives often find themselves moving from one emergency to another with the result that it is impossible to "move upstream" to establish a larger framework.

Not only does "the squeaking wheel get the oil," but the decisions made in each church to deal with the crisis have long-range consequences and cannot be reversed later if and when a larger strategy is developed. If the process goes on long enough, an area strategy becomes meaningless or impossible. The cumulative impact of individual decisions sets limits on the judicatory or congregation until planning on the basis of ideals is choked off.

The Search for New Life

An existing congregation may seek to become "new" in a number of ways. In 1971 a church in a large midwestern city woke up one day to find itself in trouble institutionally. A majority of the members, particularly the leaders, finally agreed that something had to be done. The church was losing members, the budget was more and more difficult to raise, maintenance had been deferred on the building until parts of it were beyond repair, the church school was almost nonexistent, and the worshiping congregation on Sunday morning was painfully sparse. The situation had reached the point of crisis.

The reasons for the decline were many and complex. In this case the root cause was the deterioration of the neighborhood and an influx of new people of a lower social class who did not desire to participate in its established institutions. Part of the difficulty was the church's inability to make necessary adjustments in programming and outreach.

The members were thus faced with finding an acceptable alternative if the church was to continue. In succession, various options were considered:

1. The members began to look for a "scapegoat."[1] A number of reasons were suggested for the church's decline. Some said the present pastor did not understand the congregation; others said a pastor was needed who was a better preacher. One said there was not enough programming for the youth; another pointed to the condition of the building. Finally they decided the youth were the key to the future, and they hired a part-time youth director. When this remedy did not work after a time, another solution was sought.

2. Some people left the church convinced that it was dead. Others maintained that the problem was with the membership itself and that a concerted effort must be launched in which each member would try harder. The suggestion was made that God had kept this church alive

1. See Lyle E. Schaller, *Hey, That's Our Church,* pp. 10 ff.

for these many years and would continue to sustain it if the members would do their part. All members were apprised of the critical situation facing the church and urged to increase their participation and giving.

3. When the church continued its decline, even with increased commitment, the leaders decided to turn to the denomination for help. The judicatory administrator met with the church officers and suggested several options. One option proposed and accepted was to form a cluster of several area churches for mutual support. They reasoned that several churches were duplicating many efforts, and that overhead costs could be reduced through the sharing of programs, building, and pastors. Two other churches were found, and a cooperative parish was initiated. Much to the dismay of all of the churches, however, after several months all of the congregations were becoming weaker instead of stronger as energy was diverted from the individual churches to develop and operate the parish.

4. After the cluster idea was given up and the parish disbanded, the congregation next considered relocation. The members had some knowledge of newer congregations on the periphery of the city that were doing quite well and reasoned that this church could improve its situation by moving elsewhere. After months of debate about where to move, it was evident that the congregation was severely divided on the issue and that relocation would mean a split in the congregation. The idea was given up.

5. Instead of relocation, the congregation decided, on the advice of the judicatory official to consider merger with another neighboring church. This would mean the end of the church as the members knew it, and they understood this, but they were getting desperate. Any solution that would keep the congregation together, even if other people were added, had appeal. Immediately a process of courtship with other congregations was initiated. The stronger churches were not seriously considered because they would probably not be interested in "joining us at our building," and besides "there are so many of them that our

small congregation would be swallowed up by theirs." So an equally weak congregation was found that was willing to talk about merging.

At the present time a decision has not been made. The discussions may go on for many months and, with the help of judicatory officials, the merger may finally be consummated. But even the suggestion of merger was accepted by this congregation as a breath of fresh air. It made so much sense to them that some members wondered why it was not thought of sooner. The congregation would become large again, they reasoned. "There will be more participants in worship and enough children to have a Sunday school again. Besides, merger will solve the problems of both churches at the same time." It has been rationalized that this area of the city did not really need so many churches anyway. One couple said that they know of other churches that have merged, and as far as they know, successfully. (In conversation, however, they revealed that they really do not know because their friends who attended one of the churches left at the time of merger to join a church closer to where they live.)

The present thinking of this church is that if merger does not work out with one church, they will try others. It is reasoned that other alternatives do not need to be considered because merger holds so much hope, and since no one has come up with another idea, there probably are not any others worthy of consideration.

There are three additional alternatives, but even if they were suggested, they would likely not be given serious consideration because they are not "acceptable" on their face:

1. Disband the congregation.
2. Continue for a while in recognition that the end may be in sight but that the ministry of this church will be needed for a few more years anyway.
3. Attempt to build a "new" church on the base of the "old" church that may serve an entirely different group of people in a few years and be very different than the church the present congregation wants to preserve.

It is understandable that none of these last three alternatives would be acceptable to this congregation. Any one of them would mean that the church would eventually cease to exist or be so different that most of the present members would not want to attend anyway.

The result will be an eventual painful death. Even if a merger is accomplished with another church, the results will be less desirable than those anticipated. The church failed in its efforts to find renewal for a number of reasons:

1. It did not consider all of the alternatives.

2. The church had waited too long for some of the alternatives to be possible or effective. Six of the eight alternatives could have led to a "new" church if they had been considered in time or carried out appropriately. In desperation the congregation found plausible-sounding solutions but did not analyze them fully. They were grasping at straws. In each case the same or other problems would show themselves later. It was only the immediate problems that were considered. A congregation in this condition always believes it can deal with future problems if answers can be found for the present ones.

3. The church was only concerned about itself. There was no comprehensive strategy for the denomination in which this church's problems could be evaluated.

4. Finally and most importantly, the congregation never came to grips with its motivation for wanting to continue as a church. The fact that disbanding as a congregation was never considered shows that the church did not ask whether the few remaining members might serve or be served better in other churches. The fact that becoming a different type of church was not considered shows that it was not making decisions in light of the kind of ministry now needed by the community. The purpose of the church was not a factor. The congregation was only concerned to preserve itself for those on the inside. "Whoever would save his life . . ." (Matt. 16:25, RSV).

Alternatives for Existing Congregations

The five options considered by the church in the example given here, as well as the three options that were not considered, are alternatives open to any type of church in any community. The church may be in the inner city, in an older urban or suburban residential area, on the suburban-rural fringe, in open country, or in a small town. The appropriate alternatives for a church should be decided on the basis of the present character of the community that the church serves, the internal strength of the church itself, and the point in the church's life cycle at which the situation is confronted. With this understanding of the context in which the redevelopment or renewal of existing congregations typically takes place and the patterns of thought to be expected of a church seeking to become new, we can analyze and evaluate the eight alternatives and the conditions that justify the acceptance of one or the other.

ALTERNATIVE I—STRIVE TO REGAIN PAST "SUCCESS"

There is a tendency in human nature to remember the happy moments and successes of the past and forget unhappy times and failures. The same tendency is present in congregations. The members of any congregation that has been in existence for twenty or more years typically refer often to the "good old days" and forget the struggles that preceded or accompanied them. This phenomenon is particularly strong in congregations which have declined to a point of weakness that stands in sharp contrast to the time in years gone by when the church was at its peak. The "glory" of that period has been ascribed from hindsight. Because the peak of the church occurred in conjunction with characteristics of the community that have now changed, it is impossible for the church to repeat the success of the earlier time. The church may become as successful again, but it will be successful in different ways. Alternative I is often pursued but never attained successfully.

ALTERNATIVE II—IGNORE THE PROBLEM AND HOPE IT WILL GO AWAY

Whereas Alternative I is impossible, Alternative II is unrealistic and unproductive. It is the response of the ostrich.

The fortunes of any church rise and fall with processes and events in society and in the internal life of the church. Cycles of church affiliation and participation may be noted over the course of a year or of a generation. A change of pastors or programming may cause temporary increases or decreases in participation. Thus, long-term declines are often not recognizable until they have been in progress for many years.

Further, the lay members of a congregation often do not notice membership decline until attendance at church activities drops significantly. Few members participate in all church activities. Most are not aware of decreased participation in those areas of the church's life in which they are not active.

Even when the problem becomes so severe that all active members should be aware of the trend, most are reluctant to take the responsibility of drawing it to the congregation's attention. They are afraid of the self-fulfilling prophecy. Talking about the problem may make it worse, so they ignore it and hope it will go away. It is understandable that many churches approach a point of crisis before problems are openly discussed.

Ignoring the problem with the hope that the trend will "naturally" reverse itself even after the situation is openly discussed is also a typical response in churches. Other social institutions do not do this. The belief that the church belongs to God, that He will defend and preserve it, is unique to the church. When the members do not know what to do to save the church, they put it in "God's hands." Blind faith is substituted for rational decisions and action.

I recently consulted with a neighborhood church formed five years earlier by the merger of two congregations. A study of the church revealed sharp divisions in the congregation. They were very real but never discussed. An attitudinal survey revealed that the members were divided into three groups: former members of Church A; former members of Church B, and the few members who had joined since merger. The latter group did not know what was happening. Those who had been members of one of the churches before merger knew that the division existed but would not talk about it.

When I reported the results of the survey to the congregation, a number of people became enraged. People from both former churches were united, for this one occasion at least, in recounting the efforts that had gone into making the merger work and fully believed that I had done the church a great disservice by calling "any divisions that may continue to exist" to their attention. Rather than getting the problem that was causing the church to die before the congregation so it could be dealt with, fear compelled them to ignore it in the hope that it would go away.

ALTERNATIVE III—FORM A CLUSTER WITH NEARBY CHURCHES

Cooperation among churches is highly desirable. Common participation in worship, study, fellowship, and service is to be sought, particularly in those communities where churches of the same or similar denominations serve the same parish area. There may be some projects that no one church can tackle alone, but which several churches working together can carry out successfully.

Cooperation in ministry is very different, however, than establishing common structures designed to strengthen the churches as institutions or keep them from dying. The motivation for interchurch cooperation is the critical determinant. Where the motive is to increase the outreach or service of the Church, and the participating congregations are strong enough to support adequately such a venture, success can be expected. However, "getting together" so that one or more of the churches may survive as institutions usually hastens its demise. At the very time that the congregation needs to be giving more attention to its own survival and reason for being, it creates a new structure that draws attention and resources to it.

ALTERNATIVE IV—RELOCATE

Relocation is the movement by a congregation from its building in one community to another building on a different site in the same or another community. It is initiated and carried out by congregations for a variety of reasons:

1. The church is experiencing decline in membership size, activity, and finances and cannot reverse the trend in its present setting. The desire for "success" and maintenance of a strong institution leads the group to seek "greener pastures."

2. The church is no longer needed in its present location. There are times when, as the result of urban renewal or massive changes in the community (such as one that changes from residential to industrial or commerical), the church literally has no community left. In other situations, denominational mergers may result in several churches of the same denomination having the same parish area. A church in this situation may look for another community to serve.

3. A church organized by and for a particular group of people who live in the same community may continue for a time after its former members move out of the area. For a while some of them return weekly to the church. But the new residents do not participate, and the church is of a type that cannot be converted for use by the new residents. In this case the church may relocate to be closer to its members or to seek new ones. For example, a community originally settled by Protestants may change over a few years to become predominantly Roman Catholic or Jewish. The Protestant congregation may have little chance of survival there.

4. A fire or other catastrophe may destroy a congregation's building. Those churches whose members have largely moved to other parts of the city are forced to consider relocation. The church relocates to find a site more convenient for its members or to extend its ministry.

Again, motivation is the key determinant for justifying the relocation of a particular congregation. Churches that

consider moving tend to be overly concerned with institutional survival and pay little attention to the religious
needs of the community where the congregation presently
exists. Frequently, the stated reason is not the actual reason. It is often difficult for an outsider to determine
whether the motivation is to escape problems in the
former community, or whether the church has legitimately
considered its purpose as a religious fellowship and is moving to become a new church that can continue and extend
its ministry.

To say that a church should never relocate—that it is
always escapism—is unfair. But to remove a church from a
community for the sole reason of maintaining it as an institution is unacceptable. Perhaps no congregation should
consider relocation until it has made genuine efforts to
remake and renew the church for the new residents of the
community. A church should never relocate from a community in transition when it is the only remaining church.

Aside from the motivation for relocating congregations,
there are a number of common mistakes that create problems. First, the decision is made on a unilateral basis
without sufficient consultation with other churches in the
old and new communities. Often a relocating church
moves too close to another church of the same denomination with a negative effect on both churches.

Second, relocating congregations often do not move far
enough from the old location. In an attempt to serve the
remaining members in the former community, the church
may move to a site on the edge of the former community or
to another community that is already fully developed. By
the time the relocating church is established at its new
site, the residents of the community are already involved
in other churches. The relocated church, therefore, has
difficulty recruiting as many new members as it lost when
it moved.

Third, the congregation may find that the importance of
a new building in attracting people to a church is not as
great as originally thought. Even though the congregation
may take on a heavy mortgage in order to have new facili-

ties, they may find that there are fewer people to pay for it. Churches that do not relocate wisely and under appropriate conditions rarely receive as many new members at the new location as they expect.

Fourth, the people who do not stay with the church at the time of relocation may include some of the most active and best supporting members in the church. It is rare for most members of a church to go with it to a new community and increase their commitment to it. Instead of having more resources, the church may have less.

Finally, a relocating church often fails to realize that some of the people left behind will be those who could easily get to the church at its former location but do not have transportation to the new site. Many of them may be the elderly who will have the most difficulty finding another church home.

Perhaps enough has been said to show that the relocation of a congregation is risky from an institutional point of view and may also decrease the church's potential for ministry. The high hopes usually associated with moving and the minimal results generally obtained lead to the following minimum requirements. A church may justifiably relocate if all seven of the following conditions are met:

1. If people remain in the community of the church's present location (whether members of the church or not), there are other churches of the same or similar denominations to serve the people who will continue to live there.

2. By moving to the new location, the church will not be moving away from more of its members than it is moving toward.

3. There is enthusiastic support in the congregation for the move. The decision to move should pass by a 75 percent yes vote in the congregation. In no case should less than a two-thirds majority be acceptable.

4. The area to which the church will move needs a new church of this denomination at this time whether this church relocates into it or not.

5. An adequate site in the new community can be found.

6. The church has the financial resources necessary to make the move.

7. The decision is approved as a part of a judicatory or area strategy.

In effect, then, relocation by these criteria means that an old church becomes the nucleus of a new church. Since some of the traditions of the old church are inevitably transplanted to the new, it may be better in some cases for the existing church to find another alternative and for the judicatory to start a new congregation, one with no previous existence, in the new community. There are some situations, however, in which the comprehensive strategy shows that relocation is the best action. This alternative is often appropriate when there is a community in need of a new church of this denomination, the existing church has no other acceptable alternative for finding new life itself, and many members of the existing church live in the community of the new church.

Outpost or Satellite Congregations. A new phenomenon, related both to the relocation of existing churches and the organization of new churches, is the establishment by an existing church of a satellite congregation in a new residential area. It is a combination of relocating and developing a totally new congregation, and an alternative to both.

Rather than transplant a church from one place to another, in the satellite program the existing church stays at its present location and establishes an additional congregation in a growing area of the city. The plan is similar to the new church development practice, common in several denominations, in which new congregations are sponsored by existing churches. In such cases, however, the existing church and the new church are administered separately and operate as distinct entities, at least eventually. In the satellite concept there are two congregations, but only one church, one staff, one official governing board, and one budget.

There is no intent in the satellite program of closing one

of the churches at a later time. Neither is it expected that the two congregations will be eventually combined or that the new congregation will "spin off" to become a separate church. The concept is so new, in fact, that we do not know what will result. Six Southern Baptist congregations in Texas are now experimenting with this new approach.

We may expect that in some cases the older church will close and its assets will be consolidated with the satellite congregation. Where the outpost congregation does not succeed, the two churches may merge at the older location. As some of the newer congregations grow and become strong institutions capable of self-support, they may choose to break away from the mother church with or without its blessing. Unless the older church entering into this program is prepared for such an eventuality, the schism and its aftermath may seriously impair the ministries of both congregations. On the other hand, it is possible that the two congregations can continue in the tandem relationship over long periods of time.

A variation of the satellite concept is the plan used by a number of downtown and metropolitan-regional churches. Outpost buildings are purchased in other communities for the purpose of holding meetings or providing outreach services. But there is only one congregation, and all participants are related in some way to activities at the primary location. This method of extending the ministry of a church has been very successful in a church in Little Rock, Arkansas, and in one in Wilmington, Delaware.

The new satellite concept of organizationally relating multiple congregations can have important benefits for the Church's ministry. Since the established church recruits a core group of its members to form the nucleus for the new congregation, the latter has basic support in finances, members, and lay leadership from the very beginning. Second, it is difficult to relate diverse groups of people who live in separate communities and attend different churches. In this case the congregations can be mutually supportive. For example, the community of the older congregation may provide a mission field for the new one, and the more affluent members of the congregation in the outlying area may become involved with the problems of the poor who are left in the inner-city area.

A third benefit of the satellite approach as compared to the relocation of the older church to the new community is that older members who still reside in the community are not left without a church at a time in their life when they may need it most. Finally, the satellite concept is a way of involving members of an older church in mission outreach that may have the side effect of strengthening the older church at the same time that a new mission is created. The involvement in starting the new church may provide renewed purpose to the old one and stimulate it to continue and perhaps grow.

The satellite plan also has dangers and liabilities. In the first place, the new congregation's ability to experiment may be reduced by beginning with members who have already developed a working relationship with one another and who may unthinkingly transplant structures and activities from the older church that are not appropriate in the new community. The core group may unknowingly become exclusive or reserve key positions in the new congregation for themselves. Other residents in the new community may feel that they are "latecomers," that they do not have equal standing or the freedom to help create and mold the new church. They may feel that the older congregation is paternalistic in sending in a group to start the congregation rather than assisting local residents to create their own.

Second, there is the possibility that the creation of an outpost congregation is "raw escapism" by a congregation, or cover for excessive concern with institutional survival. The real reason may be hidden by maintaining the older congregation for a time. Motivation is again the key determinant.

Third, the outpost approach can be an attempt to make legitimate what is no more than a large church, or its entrepreneur pastor, building its kingdom, or trying to secure power by expanding control over more and more congregations. Rather than the larger church accepting its responsibility of helping to coordinate and facilitate the denominational program in the area, the development of branches in the one church may result in its monopolizing the denomination in the area.

Because of its potential, and despite its limitations, the establishment of satellite congregations by existing churches is a valid area for experimentation both by existing churches wanting to help develop new congregations and by those considering relocation. When pitfalls and problems are understood ahead of time, usually they can be eliminated and helpful models created for the entire Church.

ALTERNATIVE V—MERGE WITH ANOTHER CHURCH

Merger is the uniting of two or more separate congregations into one. The new institution takes on its own attributes although the traditions and customs of the former congregations may be continued in some form.

Contrary to other institutions, mergers of churches are usually done in weakness. The constituent congregations merge because they do not have the strength to continue separately, are fast approaching that stage, or are afraid that they will someday. Merger is entered into to attain strength—not because of it. The only exception to this condition of merger among congregations is the typical situation where churches are overly concerned about institutional survival, ecumenical cooperation, or some other overriding consideration. Then it may be carried out while the churches are still strong. This does not mean, however, that strength is produced by merger.

Two churches of the same denomination in a mid-Atlantic city merged a few years ago. One had fourteen hundred members; the other had four hundred. The merger was initiated by the larger church, which had become concerned that its changing neighborhood would cause continuing membership losses. The thought of adding four hundred additional members as a hedge against such expected losses was appealing. The smaller church was persuaded to go along. Presently the newly merged church has less than thirteen hundred members and is still declining. Most of the members of the smaller church did not affiliate with the new church. Some joined other churches, but many have not affiliated with any church since the merger. If this church could see that its deteriorating condition is due more to its preoccupation with survival than any other factor, it could stop its slow decline and become a significant force in its community again.

Mergers may be attempted for a variety of reasons:

1. To attain critical mass. Churches that become so small that there are not enough people to pay the bills and fill leadership positions may merge just to have enough people to operate. Usually it does not work, and many people take the opportunity to go elsewhere. Many of those who participate in the merged church at first will later find other church homes. A newly merged church within three to five years after merger will probably have no more members than the largest church at time of merger. This being the case, if critical mass is attained at first, it will only be temporary.

2. To solve a building or clergy appointment problem. A declining church often defers building maintenance to the point where the building becomes unusable. If the church does not have the funds to pay for a new roof, a new heating unit, or to comply with the building codes of the community, or if it knows that the building is not worth the expenditure, it may seek a merger partner. In other cases a church may have difficulty securing a pastor or raising sufficient funds to pay one. This too may precipitate merger discussions.

3. To buy time so that a ministry can be continued to the remaining members for as long as possible. It is not expected here that the merger will reverse the trend and bring strength to the new congregation. It is seen only as a means of securing new life temporarily to continue a ministry as long as possible.

4. To close a church with as little pain as possible. Often

the members of a congregation who have no alternative other than disbanding will agree to merge with another church to avoid the reality of closure. Even if only a few members actually participate in the merged congregation, it is a way of transferring the assets of the dying congregation to another one. In a few cases white congregations have merged with black ones in order to transfer property.

Merger is never an ideal solution. There are a number of problems:

1. Rarely do the churches considering merger have the same community or parish area, and often they are of two different types (one may be a neighborhood church while the other is a special purpose church, for example). If the merged congregation uses the building of one of the churches, it will probably not be located near enough to serve the other community. If the churches are of different types, they may have little in common with which to build a new congregation.

2. People who have been members of a congregation for a long time have strong loyalties to it—its people, its building, its total life. Once that congregation is changed substantially, such as through merger, the attachment and loyalty may be greatly reduced, freeing the people to go to churches more conveniently located to their present residences. For this reason, it is not unusual for a newly merged congregation to have only slightly more members at the time of merger than the larger church had before. Members will probably be lost from both congregations.

3. Each church has a building, a pastor, a program, a slate of church officers, and myriads of treasured processes, which it brings to the new congregation. Whose will be kept or used? Often, this important question is overlooked until the merger has been negotiated. At some points neither congregation wants to make concessions; the compromises that are made are pleasing to no one. For example, if neither congregation is willing to sell its own building and join the other congregation at its building, they may agree to sell both buildings and build a new one.

Such a move may be unwise when viewed in terms of the life expectancy of the new congregation.

Rather than being seen as an ideal way of developing a new church, merger should be one of the last alternatives considered. Because of the poor or temporary results which may realistically be expected, it should be entered into only as a stopgap method for serving the remaining members and the communities of the churches during the time of transition. With church mergers, one plus one does not equal three. (Strength is not created out of weakness.) Further, one plus one does not equal two in church mergers. (Rarely will the new church have the combined assets of the two former churches.) But if one plus one equals one and one-half for a few years, and the only other alternative is to close one or both of the churches (zero plus zero equals zero) when a few years of service may yet be possible, then it is worth doing.

ALTERNATIVE VI—DISBAND THE CONGREGATION

Institutions are created for a purpose. Once that purpose has been fulfilled or is no longer valid, the institution is no longer needed. Congregations do not die easily, however. Because of the nature of churches, people have strong attachments to them, as well as to what they have been and done. Generally, the surviving members of a congregation at the time of its death feel guilty about its demise. Further, what remains of a particular church is still of value for the few people who are left. It is, therefore, a traumatic experience to close a church and one that is never readily accepted.

But for some churches death is inevitable. Where it cannot be faced realistically, disbanding through merger is an acceptable option. Where the remaining congregation can be led to accept it, however, the closing of the church can be a moving and uplifting celebration. Perhaps an increasing number of congregations in the future will find it possible to celebrate their church's past ministry and fulfilled goals and accept the disbanding of the congregation as the completion of a job well done, rather than as failure that produces guilt.

ALTERNATIVE VII—CONTINUE FOR A WHILE IN RECOGNITION THAT THE END MAY BE IN SIGHT

Churches which have progressively grown weak and gone past the point at which they can hope to stabilize or grow may consider all of the alternatives discussed, but find none of them acceptable or appropriate. The church is too large to disband but too small and weak to effectively pursue long-range goals. Such a church may recognize the limitations of its life but continue as long as practicable to minister to the people for whom it has responsibility. Many churches have found in this decision a release from guilt and freedom to risk that makes their last years the most productive and meaningful. Sometimes these churches find renewed purpose and many years later are still viable congregations because they were able to turn away from survival concerns to concentrate on the church's primary task.

ALTERNATIVE VIII—ATTEMPT TO BUILD A "NEW" CHURCH ON THE BASE OF THE "OLD"

Congregations that do not allow themselves to become closed systems operating apart from the environment in which they serve may find it possible in times of community transition to become new churches. These are churches that recognize the signs that point to the end of an era. They are groups of Christians who know themselves, their own ultimate concerns, and the primary task of the church. They are able to differentiate the changes in their community which take place with the ebb and flow of time and those which signal radical new crosscurrents. When they perceive the latter, they are able to reflect upon their meaning for the church. They are people who have matured in the church so that its survival is subsumed in the larger concept of purpose and task. They are willing to suffer the pains of new birth if it is demanded of them. Of course, all do not accept the change willingly, and inevitably some leave to find a comfortable pew elsewhere. But that is part of the pain. Some of the best contributors may get mad and leave too. And that brings more pain.

New life occurs for people or institutions as the consequence of death. It means giving up patterns and practices that had meaning for untried ones. It entails learning new lessons and dreaming new dreams. And that is not easy. But the church that finds new life accepts the challenge, suffers the pain, dreams of the future, and follows its Captain through the valley.

A formerly white middle-class church in a white middle-class community in an eastern city noted that their community was changing socially and racially. Sensing the need for a new church to serve the new residents who would most likely increase in the community, the congregation of almost two hundred members decided to disband, go elsewhere to church, and allow the new residents to use their facility for the organization of an indigenous church. In addition to the property, the new group also received a small endowment and the offer of continued support by some members if needed. In this case the former congregation did not intend to escape from the new residents but, recognizing the limitations inherent in one group providing a church for another group, assisted the new people to develop their own.

In another community, a former neighborhood church, acknowledging its limitations as presently constituted, discovered the need for a special purpose church to serve university students in the area and worked to make the transition possible. A number of downtown churches today have been particularly successful in recognizing the limits to their continuation as white middle-class status churches and are becoming congregations that specialize in ministries that would not be possible in neighborhood or metropolitan-regional churches.

It is never easy for a church to adjust to drastic changes

in its environment or for the members to acknowledge that another group needs "their" church more than they do. For many churches the task will be too difficult and unacceptable. But where it has been possible and acceptable in the past, new congregations have resulted and the ministry of the Church has been enhanced.

Two Perspectives

The eight alternatives discussed above represent two basic perspectives: The first is that of viewing the present state of the congregation in comparison with its past. It is exemplified by Alternatives I and II. Instead of seeking to become new, such congregations are only concerned with survival or maintaining the status quo. The results invariably are frustration and disappointment.

The second is that of viewing the present congregation in comparison with what is possible for it in the future. It is a perspective originating in the desire for new life and grows out of concern for relating people to God and empowering them for service in the world. Alternatives VI (yes, even death), VII, and VIII are examples of this view. Although painful and difficult, these options can be rewarding.

Alternatives III, IV, and V may accompany either perspective, depending upon the motivation for their acceptance. The motivation may be to escape problems, concern for survival at any cost, or genuine concern to become new.

There are no easy methods for finding the right alternative for a particular church. We can predict, however, that the alternative chosen will be the right one when it is made on the basis of an understanding of the context in which the church operates, as part of an area denominational strategy, following a feasibility study of the characteristics of the church and its community which results in probing the congregation's motivation for change, out of primary concern for ministry rather than survival, and from a perspective that is oriented to the future rather than to the past.

14 : Summary and Projections

A Look Around

Communities and churches develop and decline together. They do not exist or function apart from one another. Communities are the settings for churches; churches are the nerve centers of the communities. When one changes, the other is changed. As long as new communities are established, new churches will be needed.

The human situation cries out for answers to the questions of the purpose and ultimate meaning of life. The Christian gospel provides those answers and demands that they be shared. Historically, and until a better method is found, the local congregation is the base unit for fulfilling that mission. Some communities will not have enough churches or the appropriate types of churches unless the denominations initiate and participate in their creation. Mainline Protestant denominations and their judicatories have the experience, resources, and personnel to develop congregations that are strategic and meaningful.

Each new congregation is an opportunity for Christians to recall their own religious traditions, to organize social institutions in which those traditions may be practiced and shared. The creation of a new religious institution is an occasion to reflect, to experiment, to innovate, to participate in the establishment of a religious fellowship that can respond to the distinctive needs of the people who choose

171

to worship and serve in it. It is an opportunity for the members to symbolize and hold before the total community the participation of God in the lives of people and the fundamental need of people to share their lives and faith with one another.

The quality of a congregation's long-range ministry is related to the strength it develops during the early years of its existence. Churches allowed or forced to begin life without a clear understanding of the character of the community to be served, recognition of the primary task of the Church, and the knowledge and resources to build a strong social institution may never achieve maturity in ministry.

Developing a congregation is a long, arduous, and complex process. It requires skill and commitment, patience and hard work. Each community is unique and offers distinctive challenges. Each new church must be tailored for its environment and include the participation of a large number of people.

Each step in the new church development process affects and is affected by the other steps. The failure of the judicatory or new congregation at any point may negate or seriously impair the total effort. The judicatory has the responsibility of doing a general area survey and developing a denominational strategy for it. It selects and purchases sites, conducts feasibility studies in specific communities thought ready for new churches, prepares a preliminary mission design for each new church on the basis of its study and the distinctive characteristics of the community to be served, secures adequate financial support for the congregation, and selects a pastor who has the qualifications and commitment to lead it. The pastor is charged with the responsibility of gathering the congregation and organizing it effectively. The young congregation, together with the pastor, continues the church's outreach, evaluates and rethinks the mission design, and provides a permanent headquarters for its ministry.

The attempt has been made in this book to summarize

the experience of mainline Protestantism with regard to the process of new church development, evaluate this experience, and provide a framework that will facilitate its use in present and future efforts. It begins with the accomplishments and mistakes of a past era, reflects the state-of-the-art today, and projects goals and methods for the continuation of the process in the future.

Some of the findings represent principles that have continuing validity and broad applicability. Other procedures included here represent one acceptable way for accomplishing a task; other methods may be equally valid. Rules of thumb can be harmful rather than helpful when they are not evaluated in terms of their applicability to a particular situation. The developers of new churches who are able to draw basic axioms from this book to help them form their own framework for developing a new church, and who use specific suggestions as guidelines rather than unbreakable rules, are the ones who will create churches that are fitting and appropriate for their communities.

Simply stated we have based our discussion on the following basic principles:

1. The congregation is the basic unit of mission in the Christian Church. Failure to create new congregations in new communities is to deny a mobile population access to the one social institution that enables it to find meaning in all of life.

2. As Protestantism moves into a new wave of new church development activity, it must broaden its vision and the scope of its efforts to develop new churches in new communities wherever they may be.

3. New church development has two major foci: (a) creating a religious fellowship and (b) building a strong social institution. The former cannot exist without the latter; the latter without the former has no reason for existence.

4. The motivation for creating new congregations determines their success or failure. If the primary reason is to extend the ministry of the Church, it will rarely fail. If it is

to add members to the denomination, it cannot succeed.

5. As the development of new congregations and the redevelopment of existing congregations are interrelated, both types can be more effective. Both processes should be carried out as part of a comprehensive area strategy by the denomination.

6. All new congregations are not developed in the same mold. There are different types of churches and different forms of new congregations. The appropriate type and form for a particular church depends upon the breadth and character of its community.

7. New congregations can contribute significantly to the larger Church as they use their freedom from set patterns and traditions to build models of new forms and styles of congregational life.

8. The folly of developing ecumenical (union) congregations, except in special situations, has been proven; ecumenical cooperation among denominations in planning for the development of new congregations is essential.

9. Every congregation must have a "place" in which to gather. The type, size, style, and ownership of the building will vary by type of church.

10. The process of developing new congregations is difficult, complex, and risky. Failure to carry out an adequate program of preliminary planning, to select an experienced and qualified pastor, to locate the church where it is visible and accessible, and to provide adequate financial resources for the early years may negate the chances of building a strong institution and a mature religious fellowship.

A Look Ahead

The basic principles of new church development have been gleaned from past experiences. They will continue to provide guidelines for our efforts in the future. But perhaps the most critical decisions to be made for the last quarter of the twentieth century are related to methods and techniques that we still do not know much.about. The state-of-the-art is still cloudy in some respects.

We have learned much about style centered, ecumenical, and suburban congregations. Most of our efforts and experiments have been related to these forms, and futurists have given primary attention to the people who can be expected to participate in them.

Other forms are still new to us. Further study and experimentation is needed for intentional mission congregations, new churches for racial and ethnic groups, and congregations for the new residents of redeveloped urban areas.

As small towns and villages on the edge of metropolitan areas or in rural counties grow at an increasing rate, more small town and neighborhood churches will be needed. In areas where the increase in population is not sufficient in each town to support a new church, new metropolitan-regional churches on major transportation arteries which serve large areas will be required.

An increasing proportion of new housing in all areas will be multiple-family units. Even though many people will own their apartments, the high mobility rate will continue. Congregations that can serve these people and still maintain stability will be essential.

As the multifamily housing boom continues, there may be increasing demand for the single-family homes in the older but stable residential areas of core cities. Homogeneous communities will become heterogeneous. Urban neighborhood churches will be forced to broaden and diversify their programs and outreach or die. Many will die, and new churches will be needed to replace them. How it will be done is not yet clear.

The impersonal character of much of modern life is already changing the ways people interact and interrelate. Many people who do not participate in established churches are turning increasingly to human development groups, communes, or informal sharing fellowships. The need for intimate personal relationships and support in time of crisis, loneliness, and dependency is critical. Churches that are able to serve those needs will be in increasing demand.

The new churches of the future will be built on the experience of our historical tradition and insights into the emerging future. Our efforts inevitably take place in the present—in the uneasy tension between the two. We must be knowledgeable about both. But, in the molding of each new church we will make new breakthroughs and new mistakes, discover new models and discard old ones. We will succeed and we will fail.

But success is not our goal. The test of our discipleship is our faithfulness. The future is in God's hands. The Church is his creation, and He will judge its success. Meanwhile

> the mainstream of the Church's life goes on in the parish church and local congregation. Were this to be abandoned, it is doubtful that much else would survive.[1]

1. Georgia Harkness, *Stability Amid Change*, p. 30.

Selected Bibliography

Anderson, James D., *To Come Alive* (New York: Harper & Row, Publishers, 1973).

DeBoer, John C., and Greendale, Alexander, eds., *Are New Towns for Lower Income Americans Too?* (New York: Praeger Publishers, 1974).

"Designing Today's Congregations—Guidelines for Cooperative Strategies," a leaflet prepared by the Joint Strategy and Action Committee.

Dulles, Avery, S.J., *Models of the Church* (Garden City: Doubleday & Company, Inc., 1974).

Frazier, E. Franklin, *The Negro Church in America* (New York: Schoken Press, 1973).

Gans, Herbert J., *The Levittowners* (New York: Pantheon Books, 1967).

Harkness, Georgia, *Stability Amid Change* (Nashville: Abingdon Press, 1969).

Jones, Ezra Earl, ed., *New Church Development in the Eighties—Some Perspectives from the Seventies* (New York: The United Methodist Board of Global Ministries, 1976).

Jones, Ezra Earl, and Wilson, Robert L., *What's Ahead for Old First Church* (New York: Harper & Row, Publishers, 1974).

Journal of Small Business Management, January 1972.

Kelley, Dean M., *Why Conservative Churches Are Growing* (New York: Harper & Row, Publishers, 1972).

Lippitt, Gordon L., *Organization Renewal* (New York: Appleton-Century-Crofts, 1969).

Metz, Donald L., *New Congregations* (Philadelphia: The Westminster Press, 1967).

Olsen, Charles M., *The Base Church* (Atlanta: Forum House/Publishers, 1973).

Park, Philip K. S., "Factors in Racial Church Development," a chapter in *New Church Development in the Eighties,* edited by Ezra Earl Jones (New York: The United Methodist Board of Global Ministries, 1976).

Reed, Bruce, "The Task of the Church and the Role of Its Members" (London: The Grubb Institute, 1975), a paper based on the Keene Lecture delivered at Chelmsford Cathedral, England, November, 1974.

Sarason, Seymour B., *The Creation of Settings and the Future Societies* (San Francisco: Jossey-Bass Publishers, 1972).

Schaller, Lyle E., *Hey, That's Our Church* (Nashville: Abingdon Press, 1975).

Smith, H. Paul, and Jones, Ezra Earl, *The Church Building Process* (New York: The United Methodist Board of Global Ministries, 1975).

Sovik, E. A., *Architecture for Worship* (Minneapolis: Augsburg Publishing House, 1973).

Stackhouse, Max L., *Ethics and the Urban Ethos* (Boston: Beacon Press, 1972).